Taking the Mystery Out of Virginia School Finance

Financing Public Elementary and Secondary Education in the Commonwealth of Virginia

Richard G. Salmon

M. David Alexander

NCPEA Publications

National Council of Professors of Educational Administration

Ypsilanti, Michigan

Published by NCPEA Publications

The publications of the National Council of Professors of Educational Administration (NCPEA)
http://www.ncpeapublications.org

Printed in United States of America

Library of Congress Cataloging-in-Publication Data

Salmon, Richard G. and Alexander, M. David,
Taking the mystery out of Virginia school finance: Financing elementary and secondary education in the Commonwealth of Virginia

ISBN 978-1-4951-1150-1 (pbk)

How to order this book:

NCPEA Press, a book publisher for NCPEA Publications offers *Taking the Mystery Out of Virginia School Finance* as a Print-on-Demand hard copy or eBook at: http://www.ncpeapublications.org

Printed Books are prepared in Perfect Bound binding and delivery is 3-5 days. eBooks are delivered to one's computer or other reading device in minutes.

Taking the Mystery Out of Virginia School Finance has been peer reviewed, accepted, and endorsed by the National Council of Professors of Educational Administration as a significant contribution to the preparation and practice of school administration.

NCPEA Press Director and Editor, Theodore B. Creighton

NCPEA Publications Director and Technical Editor, Brad E. Bizzell

Cover Design by Brad E. Bizzell; Cover photograph by Mike Kaylor, teacher at Blacksburg High School, Blacksburg, Virginia

Table of Contents

Array of Figures and Charts

CHAPTER 1

Introduction

To understand fully how public schools in the United States and the Commonwealth of Virginia are financed, one must have knowledge of the legal structure and organization of public education. There are approximately 15,800 school districts in the United States, which vary in size, and for the most part have small student enrollments. Approximately 55 percent of the districts enroll less than 1,000 pupils while 90 percent have 5,000 or fewer pupils.[1] Also, the titles of school districts vary among the states. For example, the federal government refers to local school districts as *Local Education Agencies, (LEAs)* while Louisiana titles their LEAs as *parishes.* Indiana names their LEAs *corporations* and Virginia titles their LEAs, *school divisions.* For the purpose of consistency, the authors of this manual refer to the LEAS as *school districts.* Some states, including the Commonwealth of Virginia, also have several of their school districts classified as *non-operating*, such as the Fairfax City Public Schools, which has entered into a long term contract with Fairfax County Public Schools to provide educational services for students from Fairfax City. Shown in **Appendix A** is the numbers of school districts per state, operating and non-operating, for School Year, 2013-2014. Hawaii has a centralized state education system and therefore reported only one school district. Texas reported the largest number of school districts, 1,299. The reason for this great variance among state educational systems is that the U.S. Constitution makes no mention of education. The 10th Amendment of the U.S. Constitution states:

> The powers not delegated to the United States by the Constitution, nor prohibited
> by it to the States, are reserved to the States respectively, or to the people.

The Federal government can only do what is explicit or implied by the U.S. Constitution; since education is not mentioned, it becomes the jurisdiction of the states. Also, there is a legal difference in interpreting the Federal Constitution as opposed to individual state constitutions. While the Federal government may only do what the U.S. Constitution allows explicitly or implicitly, the states may do anything that is not prohibited by the U.S. Constitution or their own state constitutions. This legal difference between the U.S. and State Constitutions was articulated in *Commonwealth v. Hartman*, when the court stated:

> It is to be remembered, that the rule of interpretation for the state constitution
> differs totally from that which is applicable to the Constitution of the United
> States. The latter instrument must have a strict construction; the former a liberal
> one . . . Congress can pass no laws but those which the Constitution authorizes
> either expressly or by clear implication; while the assembly [state] has jurisdiction
> of all subjects on which its legislation is not prohibited. The powers, not granted

---

[1] U.S. Department of Education, National Center for Education Statistics, *Public School Data File.* (Washington, D.C.: NCES, 2007-2008).

to the government of the Union, are withheld; but the state retains every attribute of sovereignty which is not taken away. [2]

Since education is not *explicitly* mentioned in the U.S. Constitution, the question arises: *Is it implied?* The U.S. Supreme Court in *San Antonio Independent School District v. Rodriguez*, (1973) addressed education and the U.S. Constitution and stated: *...the answer lies in assessing whether there is a right to education explicitly or implicitly guaranteed by the Constitution.*[3] The Court reiterated the importance of education by citing the following statement in the unanimous 1954 *Brown v. Board of Education* decision:

> Education is perhaps the most important function of state and local government . . . Education is not only important to our society - it is vital to a free society.[4]

In *Rodriquez*, the Supreme Court recognized the importance of education in the engagement of political dialogue and free speech and noted that if you are *ill-fed, ill-clothed and ill-housed,*[5] then these conditions would also impede your efforts in the political process. However, the court found that education was neither an explicit nor implicit right under the Federal Constitution.[6][7] In essence, the court reinforced the doctrine that the legal responsibility for the provision of public education rests with the states.

In the United States, there are 50 state educational systems and 50 unique school finance systems. This diversity includes all aspects of public education, including the derivation and appropriation of revenue to operate the schools. All states, except Iowa, have enacted education clauses in their state constitutions. Two sections in the 1971 Virginia Constitution directly address the responsibilities of the Commonwealth pursuant to the provision of public schools.

> § 1. Public schools of high quality to be maintained
>
> The General Assembly shall provide for a system of free public elementary and secondary schools for all children of school age throughout the Commonwealth, and shall seek to ensure that an educational program of high quality is established and continually maintained.[8]

---

[2] 17 PA. 118, (1851).

[3] 411 US at 53, 93 S.Ct. 1297

[4] 347 US at 493, 74 S.Ct. at 691

[5] 411US at 36, 93 S.Ct. at 1297-1298

[6] Drawn from *San Antonio Independent school District v. Rodriguez*, 411 US at 30, 93 S.Ct. at 1295.

[7] This theme, expressing an abiding respect for the vital role of education in a free society, may be found in numerous opinions of the Supreme Court, writing both before and after *Brown* was decided. See for example, *Wisconsin v. Yoder*, 406 U.S. 205, 213, 92 S.Ct. 1526, 1532, (1972); *Abington School Dist. v. Schempp*, 374 U.S. 203, 230, 83 S.Ct. 1560, 1575; *People of State of Illinois ex rel. McCollum v. Board of Education*, 333 U.S. 203, 212, 68 S.Ct. 461, 465; *Pierce v. Society of Sisters*, 268 U.S. 510, 45 S.Ct. 571, (1925); *Meyer v. Nebraska*, 262 U.S. 390, 43 S.Ct. 625, (1923).

[8] *VA Const. Art. 8, § 1 Constitution of Virginia* [1971]

§ 2. Standards of quality; State and local support of public schools.

Standards of quality for the several school districts shall be determined and prescribed from time to time by the Board of Education, subject to revision only by the General Assembly.

The General Assembly shall determine the manner in which funds are to be provided for the cost of maintaining an education program meeting the prescribed standards of quality, and shall provide for the apportionment of the cost of such program between the Commonwealth and the local units of government comprising such school districts. Each unit of local government shall provide its portion of such cost by local taxes or from other available funds.[9]

Additionally, education is contained in the Virginia Bill of Rights:

That free government rests, as does all progress, upon the broadest possible diffusion of knowledge, and that the Commonwealth should avail itself of those talents which nature has sown so liberally among its people by assuring the opportunity for their fullest development by an effective system of education throughout the Commonwealth.[10]

The structure of public schools differ among states, including compulsory attendance, school district organization, selection of school board members, and the method of funding the public schools. Each state makes policy decisions regarding whether the revenue will be generated at the state or local levels, and the taxes that will be used to generate the revenue. Displayed in Table 1 are the percentages of revenue for schools provided by the three levels of government, local, state, and federal.[11] Nationally, for FY 2011, the percentages of revenues, by source, were: 43.4% local, 44.1% state, and 12.5 % federal. Note that Illinois provided 57.8% from local sources, while Vermont provided only 7.6% local funds. In contrast, Vermont provided 81.7% from state sources, while Illinois provided 32.2%. Among the fifty states, South Dakota provided the smallest percentage from state sources, 29.1%. The variances in the percent of revenue provided by source illustrate the different philosophies for funding public schools that are held by the citizens of the fifty states. However, those states that provide low percentages of state revenue usually have significant per pupil expenditure disparities among their school districts.

---

[9] VA Const. Art. 8, § 2 Constitution of Virginia [1971]
[10] VA Const. Art. 1, § 15 Constitution of Virginia [1971]
[11] U.S. Department of Education, National Center for Education Statistics, *Selected Statistics From the Common Core of Data: School Year 2011–12.* (Washington, D.C.: NCES, 2013).

TABLE 1:   Percent of Revenue for Public Elementary and Secondary Education from Local, State & Federal Sources: (FY 2011)

State	% Local	% State	% Federal
Alabama	31.2	51.8	16.9
Alaska	21.1	61.7	17.2
Arizona	43.0	40.2	16.8
Arkansas	32.5	51.3	16.3
California	29.8	56.6	13.6
Colorado	48.6	40.1	11.2
Connecticut	57.5	34.3	8.3
Delaware	29.5	58.6	11.9
Florida	47.4	34.4	18.2
Georgia	45.5	41.7	12.8
Hawaii	2.6	83.4	14.1
Idaho	22.7	63.3	14.0
Illinois	57.8	32.2	10.0
Indiana	35.5	55.6	8.9
Iowa	46.4	43.2	10.4
Kansas	35.8	52.5	11.7
Kentucky	31.8	51.8	16.4
Louisiana	39.2	42.2	18.6
Maine	48.4	40.5	11.1
Maryland	49.7	41.0	9.3
Massachusetts	54.0	37.8	8.3
Michigan	31.0	55.1	13.9
Minnesota	33.2	58.5	8.3
Mississippi	31.3	46.2	22.4
Missouri	56.8	29.6	13.6
Montana	38.2	43.7	18.1
Nebraska	53.5	30.3	16.2
Nevada	56.0	33.0	11.0
New Hampshire	56.2	36.6	7.2
New Jersey	57.4	37.3	5.3
New Mexico	16.0	64.7	19.3
New York	50.5	40.1	9.3
North Carolina	25.7	58.1	16.2
North Dakota	35.1	50.0	14.8

State	% Local	% State	% Federal
Ohio	45.0	43.2	11.8
Oklahoma	36.2	46.9	16.9
Oregon	40.2	45.6	14.1
Pennsylvania	53.3	34.5	12.2
Rhode Island	52.6	36.4	11.0
South Carolina	42.8	43.4	13.8
South Dakota	50.6	29.1	20.3
Tennessee	40.5	44.8	14.7
Texas	44.2	40.2	15.7
Utah	36.5	50.9	12.6
Vermont	7.6	81.7	10.7
Virginia	53.1	37.0	9.9
Washington	31.2	57.3	11.6
West Virginia	29.5	55.8	14.7
Wisconsin	44.9	45.9	9.1
Wyoming	37.2	53.3	9.4
United States	43.4	44.1	12.5

Source: *Ibid.*

A question often asked is: *If the U.S. Constitution limits Congress to do only what is explicit or implied in the Constitution, by what authority does the federal government legally spend money for K-12 public education?*

The U.S. Supreme Court ruled in the 1937 *Helvering v. Davis* decision that congress has wide latitude to determine what constitutes the *general welfare*. The court found that the Social Security Act of 1935 was constitutional under the *General Welfare Clause* and stated:

> Congress may spend money in aid of the *general welfare* U.S Constitution, Art.1, §8. The line must still be drawn between one welfare and another, between particular and general. Where this shall be placed cannot be known through a formula in advance of the event. The discretion, however, is not confided to the courts. The discretion belongs to Congress, unless the choice is clearly wrong, a display of arbitrary power, nor an exercise of judgment. This is now familiar law. "When such a contention comes here we naturally require a showing that by no reasonable possibility can the challenged legislation fall within the wide range of discretion permitted to the Congress. Nor is the concept of the *general welfare* static. Needs that were narrow or parochial a century ago may be interwoven in our day with the well-being of the nation. What is critical or urgent changes with the times.

The purge of nationwide calamity that began in 1929 has taught us many lessons. Not the least is the solidarity of interests that may once have seemed to be divided. Unemployment spreads from state to state, the hinterland now settled that in pioneer days gave an avenue of escape. … Spreading from state to state, unemployment is an ill not particular but general, which may be checked, if Congress so determines, by the resources of the nation. The hope behind this statute is to save men and women from the rigors of the poor house as well as from the haunting fear that such a lot awaits them when journey's end is near.[12]

Thus, the federal government provides funds to K-12 education through the *General Welfare Clause*, also known as the *Spending Powers Clause*. The Constitution states:

The Congress shall have Power to lay and collect Taxes, Duties, Imposts and Excises, to pay the Debts and provide for the common Defence and general Welfare of the United States; but all Duties, Imposts and Excises shall be uniform throughout the United States[13]

The largest federal program for education is the venerable *Elementary and Secondary Education Act of 1965,* now titled the *No Child Left Behind Act of 2001*, which is funded through the above *Spending Clause Act* of the U.S. Constitution. Any act passed under the *Spending Clause* is basically a contract; for example, if the school district accepts federal funds, it is obligated to follow the federal guidelines. A recent law review article addressed the *No Child Left Behind Act* and stated:

Congress has passed legislation [previously] on education and conditioned federal spending on the institution of federal educational objectives. The largest and most recent example of Congress using its power under the Spending Clause to shape nationwide educational policy came with the passage of No Child Left Behind (NCLB) [Act] in 2001. NCLB is an expansive educational program that conditions the acceptance of federal funds for education on the states' implementation of a system of accountability for students, teachers, and schools . . . . The entire program of NCLB is based on Congress's authority under the Spending Clause to attach conditions to funds given to the states.[14]

Additionally, the Supreme Court stated, in *South Dakota v. Elizabeth H. Dole Secretary, U.S. Department Transportation*, that the proper legal interpretation of the Spending Powers Clause was:

The spending power is of course not unlimited . . . The first of these limitations is derived from the language of the Constitution itself: the exercise of the spending power must be in pursuit of "the general welfare" . . . In considering whether a particular expenditure is intended to serve general public purposes, courts should defer substantially to the judgment of Congress . . . Second, we have required that

---

[12] 301 US 672 at 640-641, 57 S.Ct. 904, at 908.
[13] *United States Constitution, Article I, § 8.*
[14] Snyder, Christine, *Reversing the Tide: Restoring First Amendment Ideals in America's Schools Through Legislative Protections for Journalism Students and Advisors,* 2014 B.Y.U. Educ. & L.J. 71.

if Congress desires to condition the States' receipt of federal funds, it "must do so unambiguously . . . enabl[ing] the States to exercise their choice knowingly, cognizant of the consequences of their participation . . . [T]he Federal Government may establish and impose reasonable conditions relevant to federal interest in the project and to the over-all objectives thereof.[15]

States have the responsibility for determining their own educational policies; but if they do accept federal dollars, they must comply with the legislative requirements of the federal statute or risk the loss of federal funds.

Fiscally Independent or Fiscally Dependent School Districts

In the United States, school districts are either fiscally dependent or fiscally independent. Those school boards which are fiscally independent have the authority to develop a budget and levy taxes for their budgetary needs. Nationally, the majority of school boards are fiscally independent. Normally, fiscally independent school boards elect, rather than appoint their school board members.[16] In 1992, the Virginia General Assembly passed legislation that permits local jurisdictions to conduct referenda to determine whether to elect or continue to appoint their local school board members.[17] As displayed in **Appendix B**, most Virginia localities have chosen to elect members of their school boards. However, regardless of whether the local school boards are elected or appointed, they remain fiscally dependent.

Fiscally independency falls in three categories: 1) purely independent, where the board develops the budget and levies the tax rate; 2) independent with tax limitations, if the school board needs revenue above the tax limitation, a referendum is needed to increase the tax rate; and 3) similar to category 2, but titled a *town hall model*, generally found in New England, where the citizens meet to approve the school board budget and set the local tax rate.[18]

Virginia's school districts are fiscally dependent upon the local governing bodies, both county boards of supervisors and city councils. The local school superintendent is responsible, with the approval of the local school board, for the preparation and submission of the annual school budget to the governing bodies.[19] The governing bodies have been given the authority by the General Assembly to have near complete fiscal control over local school budgets.

---

[15] 483 U.S. 203 at 207-208, 107 S.Ct. 2793 at 2796, (1987).

[16] Tennessee School Boards Association, *Elected School Boards and Fiscal Authority.*(Nashville, TN: TSBA, 2007).

[17] Code of Virginia, Article 7. §22.1-57.1. POPULAR ELECTION OF SCHOOL BOARD, **Applicability.**

[18] Lunenburt, Fred C., *North Carolina School Board Association and the School District Budget.* (Huntsville, TX: Sam Houston State University Schooling, Vol. 1, No. 1, 2010).,

[19] Code of Virginia, §22.1-92, **Estimate of moneys needed for public schools; notice of costs to be distributed.**

Revenue Sources

The next question is: *From where do these revenues for funding public schools come?* Local revenues generally come from property taxes; state revenues are generated from taxes on income, both individual and corporate, and sales taxes; federal revenue is collected from individual and corporate income taxes and from a myriad of other taxes, such as, motor fuel, alcohol, tobacco and others.

In the Commonwealth of Virginia, cities, counties and towns administer several taxes and rates differ from jurisdiction to jurisdiction. Local governments use four major taxes, real estate tax, tangible personal property, utility taxes, and sales and use taxes. In some real estate instances, taxes are collected by specific districts within counties; an example is furnished by Fairfax County, which has an extensive list of additional district property tax rates ranging from 0.001 to 0.406 per $100 of assessed valuation. Some localities impose a local excise tax on cigarettes, admissions, room rentals and food. The major taxes on corporations are real estate, machinery and tools.[20]

Property Tax

Property taxes are classified as real or personal and are levied at uniform rates on all tangible and intangible property located within the school district. Real property is predominantly land, buildings, and improvements; whereas tangible personal property includes other forms of property, such as, computers, cattle, cars, machinery, etc. Intangible personal property includes items such as, stocks and bonds. Some distinguish between real and personal property as fixed versus movable.

The real property tax is an *ad valorem* tax, meaning *to the value*; the tax amount is set according to the value of the property. It is also an *ad rem* tax which means it is levied on the property and not the owner. Property taxation is an old method of raising funds primarily because of its' distinguishable characteristic of being easy to locate and tax. Critics of the real property tax often complain that it is regressive,[21] since the tax rate is the same whether the property is a modest bungalow or a mansion; however, it has been a reliable source of local revenue since colonial days, and it is not nearly as regressive as the more popular sales tax.

Tangible personal property, as mentioned earlier, can be touched and is movable. All states, except Oklahoma, exempt personal property which is not used for producing income, such as household items like furniture and jewelry; however, Oklahoma does use the personal property tax in six of its 77 counties.[22] Some states levy taxes on motor vehicles, boats, airplanes, and other licensed items classified as tangible personal property, while others tax these items through use of excise taxes. Among the fifty states, tangible personal property varies from 5% to 15% of total state and local assessed value of property. Requirements for reporting tangible personal property require owners to submit tax forms that list their tangible personal property; however,

---

[20] Commonwealth of Virginia, *Virginia Tax Facts*. (Richmond, VA: Department of Taxation, January 2014).

[21] A *regressive* tax is defined as a tax where the tax rate declines as the tax base increases. In contrast, a *progressive* tax is defined as a tax where the tax rate increases as the tax base increases.

[22] The Tax Foundation has indicated that states are moving away from levying taxes on tangible personal property, excluding taxes levied on licensed vehicles, Oct. 4, 2012.

these forms are often burdensome, and since states generally have low audit rates, the result are high rates of tax evasion. Therefore, states have moved away from use of tangible personal property as a revenue source, other than taxes on licensed items, because of administrative difficulties and disincentives for individuals and businesses to accurately report their property.

An example of the Virginia tax on tangible personal property is provided by Montgomery County, Virginia. In the Commonwealth of Virginia, Commissioners of the Revenue assess tangible personal property while the County Boards of Supervisors establish the tax rates per $100 assessed value. Assessment is based on ownership and/or the *situs*[23] of property on January 1st each year. Rates for Montgomery County, Virginia in CY 2014 were: (PP) personal property - $2.55, (MV) Motor Vehicle - $2.55, (BF) Business Furniture & Fixtures - $ 2.55, (CE) Computer Equipment (for business) - $2.55, (MC) Merchants Capital - $3.05, (MT) Machinery & Tools -$ 1.82 , (AC) Air Craft - $1.23 and (MH) Mobile Home -$0.89.

Sales Tax

Sales taxes are used by the states and federal government to collect significant revenue. Nationally, it the primary revenue source for state governments, and it is by far the most regressive of the major taxes. Forty-five states have enacted statewide sales taxes; in addition, 38 states have authorized their local governments to levy sales taxes. The five highest state sales taxes for combined state and local governments are: Tennessee (9.45%), Arkansas (9.19%), Louisiana (8.89%), Washington (8.8%) and Oklahoma (8.72%). The five states that do not use sales taxes are: Alaska, Montana, Oregon, New Hampshire and Delaware.

California has the highest state rate (7.5%); whereas 5 states have a 7% rate (Indiana, Mississippi, New Jersey, Rhode Island and Tennessee); Colorado has the lowest rate – at 2.9%. Virginia has a 5.3% combined state and local sales tax rate with localities in Northern Virginia and Hampton Roads charging a combined 6% (5.3% state and .7% local). However, Shown in **Appendix** C are the combined state and local sales taxes for the Commonwealth as of January 1, 2014. It should be noted that Virginia returns annually a dedicated 1.0% of sales tax receipts to the localities for public schools. Additionally, 1.0% of sales tax receipts is collected and remains with the localities, leaving the remaining 3.3% for use by the Commonwealth.

Income Tax

In 1894, Congress passed the *Wilson – Gorman Act* that *levied 2% on income of $4,000, plus it was applied to gains, profits, dividends, or salaries . . . to both individuals and corporations.* The act was challenged in *Pollock v. Framers' Loan & Trust Co.*[24] The U.S. Supreme Court by a 5-4 vote ruled the entire *Wilson – Gorman Act* unconstitutional on grounds that an income tax was a direct tax and must be levied in proportion to the population of the states. In 1913, the U.S. Constitution was amended to include the 16th Amendment, which states:

---

[23] In law, the **situs** is the site of property, or the location of property for legal purposes.
[24] 158 U.S. 601, 15S.Ct. 912, (1895).

The Congress shall have power to lay and collect taxes on income, from whatever source derived, without apportionment among the several states, and without regard to any census or enumeration.[25]

The income tax is now used by both federal and state governments (and, in some states, local governments) to collect revenue. There are seven states that have declined to implement state income taxes (Alaska, Florida, Nevada, South Dakota, Texas, Washington and Wyoming); additionally, two states, Tennessee and New Hampshire, have levied such a modest tax on income that it is classified as *nearly no income tax.* Tennessee has a *hall tax* which is a 6% levy on interest and dividends, permissible by the State Constitution; its legislature may also tax property and income from stocks and bonds, but is prohibited from levying a tax on individual income. New Hampshire also has no income tax, but allows a 5% tax on interest and dividends. Also, New Hampshire does not levy a sales tax, but does derive revenue from the 8.5% corporate tax, as well as from the levy of very high real property taxes.

The Commonwealth of Virginia has a state income tax; its calculation is shown in **Table 2** below. Additionally, the Commonwealth collects a 6% flat rate corporate income tax.[26] The Commonwealth prohibits localities from levying a local income tax:

> No county, city, town or other political subdistrict of this Commonwealth shall impose any tax or levy upon incomes, incomes being hereby segregated for state taxation only.[27]

TABLE 2: Calculation of the Virginia Income Tax[28]

If Taxable Income is:			
Over	**But not over**	**Tax is**	**Of excess over**
$0	$3,000	2%	
$3,000	$5,000	$60+3%	$3,000
$5,000	$17,000	$120+5%	$5,000
$17,000		$720+5.75%	$17,000

Seventeen states impose a local income tax. In Indiana and Maryland, all counties have levied local income taxes, as do 181 Ohio school districts and 469 Pennsylvania school districts. Among the fifty states, a vast array of taxes have been developed and levied, including the so-

---

[25] Passed by Congress on July 2, 1909, and ratified February 3, 1913.
[26] http://taxfoundation.org/state-tax-climate/
[27] §58.1-300. **Incomes not subject to local taxation.**
[28] Virginia Department of Taxation, *Virginia Tax Facts.* (Richmond, VA: Commonwealth of Virginia, January 2014). Retrieved from: http://www.tax.virginia.gov/Documents/TaxFacts.pdf.

called, *Jock Tax*, which is a local income tax levied on professional athletes. Several states tax visiting musicians, lawyers, and professional skateboarders, according to the Tax Foundation. This practice has been labeled a very poor tax policy because it is arbitrarily enforced and presents a difficult administrative burden. Tennessee recently repealed its *Jock Tax* as applied to National Hockey League players, effective immediately; but the tax remains in effect for the National Basketball Association players until 2016. Apparently loved by the Tennessee legislature, Tennessee also has exempted National League Football players from the *Jock Tax*.[29] An example of the arbitrariness of this tax is furnished by the plight of former NFL player, Jeff Saturday, who recently lost a tax assessment appeal to the City of Cleveland, Ohio. Saturday, who played for the Indianapolis Colts, was injured and did not travel to a game in Cleveland. Nevertheless, the tax court ruled that he was still required to pay the *Jock Tax*.[30]

Summary

The purpose of this chapter was to give the reader a legal and practical context to public school finance in the United States. When studying how a state's public schools are financed, it must be remembered that the method of funding is unique to each state, and in most states, the systems of school finance are complicated. The following chapters address specifically the system of school finance employed by the Commonwealth of Virginia.

---

[29] Chris Stephens, *Tennessee Jock Finally Socked.* (New York: Tax Foundation, April 15, 2014).
[30] *Ohio Board of Tax Appeals Tackles Jock Tax Challenges with Saturday . . .* (New York: National Tax Foundation, Feb. 7, 2014), *Ibid.*

CHAPTER 2

An Historical Review of the Virginia System for Financing Public Schools

Public elementary and secondary education, a vast, uneven and complex system, is the most significant cost to local government and one of the largest costs to state government in Virginia. Meeting this cost has become even more difficult as the state and nation continue to struggle with the aftermath of the most severe recession since the *Great Depression* of the 1930s. This extended economic downturn is often labeled the *Great Recession* which commenced for the United States in December, fourth quarter of 2007. The nation did not emerge from the *Great Recession* until June, second quarter of 2009; but, while most major industries have or are in the process of recovering from the recession, labor has continued to struggle. Most economists now consider that the United States has entered a period of sustained economic recovery, and some indicators suggest that substantial progress has been made toward full recovery. For example, the stock market and corporate profits have both surpassed their pre-recession peak.[31] However, less than fifty percent of households invest in the stock market, even including stock held indirectly in their retirement accounts. Even among those households that do hold stock, they possess less than meaningful amounts; less than one-third own stock worth a minimum of $10,000.[32]

Most states, including the Commonwealth of Virginia, felt an even tighter financial pinch when the infusion of federal stimulus funding ceased. In light of these pressures, presented in Chapter 1 is an historical background of public school funding in Virginia. Also presented are descriptions of the complicated and controversial formulae used to allocate state funds to local school districts for the support of public elementary and secondary education.

Early Years

The Commonwealth of Virginia, similar to other southern states, was not an early supporter of public schools, often referred to as *common schools*, during the colonial years and well into the twentieth century. Despite the urging of Thomas Jefferson, John Tyler, and other Virginians, the state was slow to subscribe to the notion of free public education. An historical study of the *Virginia Literary Fund*,[33] which was enacted initially and feebly to educate the poor, found that the main barrier for the establishment of a state-supported system of common schools was the attitudes of the people themselves.[34] A study by Thayer concluded,

---

[31] Measured in constant dollars, i.e. inflation has been taken into consideration through use of the Consumer Price Index.

[32] Mishel, Lawrence, Josh Bivens, Elise Gould, and Heidi Shierholz. *The State of Working America, 12th Edition.* An Economic Policy Institute Book. (Ithaca, N.Y.: Cornell University Press, 2012).

[33] *Constitution of Virginia, (1971)*, Article VIII, §8 and *Code of Virginia (1950)*, §§22.1-142 to 22.1-161. **Literary Fund.**

[34] Mullins, Foney G., *A History of the Literary Fund as a Funding Source for Free Public Education in the Commonwealth of Virginia.* Ed.D., Dissertation. (Blacksburg, Virginia: Virginia Tech, 2001).

The economic and social system in the South consisting of an aristocratic upper class, a relatively weak middle class, "poor whites," free Negroes, and on the lowest level, slaves, was unfavorable to the development of publicly supported free schools. Such development is more characteristic of a society composed of free labor and a vigorous middle class.[35]

Prior to the enactment of the Virginia Literary Fund in 1810, the General Assembly made virtually no state appropriations for common schools, and the localities provided only the most meager fiscal support. Since its establishment, the Literary Fund has been used for several purposes, including its initial objective of providing a minimal education for the poorest white children. Ultimately, the Literary Fund evolved into a loan mechanism that provides low-interest loans to local school districts for the construction of school facilities and periodically helps balance the state general fund during economic recessions. The Literary Fund was linked more recently to the Virginia Public School Authority (VPSA) in order to finance other capital needs of the public schools, including computer technology. The Virginia Literary Fund initially was financed by fines, forfeitures, penalties, confiscations, escheats and debt repayment for the War of 1812.[36] The current Literary Fund receives its revenues similarly,

> …the proceeds of all public lands donated by Congress for free public school purposes, of all escheated property, of all waste and unappropriated lands, of all property accruing to the Commonwealth by forfeiture except as hereinafter provided, of all fines collected for offenses committed against the Commonwealth, and of the annual interest upon the Literary Fund; and such other sums as the General Assembly may appropriate.[37]

Ostensibly, Literary Fund appropriations were to be expended exclusively for public schools. However, since its inception, Literary Fund resources have been diverted to other state purposes, including an early diversion of funds to help establish the University of Virginia.[38] Much more recently in 1990, a constitutional amendment was ratified that diverted permanently a portion of Literary Fund revenues. Revenues derived from property seized and forfeited pursuant to criminal drug violations are now designated for law enforcement.[39] Because of the diversion of funds, unstable revenue streams, and insufficient appropriations, by the mid-1800s, the Literary Fund was incapable of providing sufficient financial resources to establish and maintain an adequate system of free public schools throughout the state. The initial reluctance of the body politic to fund public schools through taxation, particularly from state resources, proved difficult to overcome; however, it did provide a much-needed starting point for subsequent development of a comprehensive system for financing universal public education. Through the General Assembly, supporters of public schools attempted to enact a system of free universal education in 1829[40] and again in 1846,[41] but neither attempt resulted in legislation that required either the state or localities to provide sufficient public revenue to operate or maintain a system of public

---

[35]Thayer, V.T., *Formative Ideas in American Education.* (New York: Dodd, Mead & Company, Inc., 1965) at 69.
[36] Mullins, *Supra* at 32
[37]*Constitution of Virginia, (1971)*, Article VIII, §8.
[38]*Acts of Virginia Assembly of the Commonwealth of Virginia, (1818).*
[39] *Constitution of Virginia (1971) Supra.*
[40] *Acts of Virginia Assembly of the Commonwealth of Virginia, (1829),* Supra.
[41] *Ibid., (1846).*

schools. In the years leading up to the Civil War and during the war years, 1861 to 1865, there was even less movement toward the establishment of a viable system of public education.

Reconstruction Period

During the reconstruction period following the Civil War, Virginia was burdened with a destroyed infrastructure, an economic system in shambles, and a largely uneducated or undereducated population. In the midst of this chaotic environment, a constitutional convention was convened in 1867, and New York Judge John C. Underwood was named as its' president. Thus, a newly-written *Virginia Constitution*, that became effective in 1870, is often entitled the *Underwood Constitution*. Contained within the Underwood Constitution, for the first time, was the inclusion of an article that required the General Assembly to provide compulsory and universal free public education.[42] State revenues were derived from Literary Fund investments, a capitation tax (a tax levied upon individuals, also called head tax), and a statewide property tax of not less than one mill and not more than five mills on the dollar. In contemporary Virginia terminology that translates to not less than $0.10 per $100 of assessed value and not more than $0.50 per $100 of assessed value.[43] Funds were allocated to each free public school district based upon the number of children aged 5-21 years. Although not mandated, each county and public free school district could levy additional millage not to exceed five mills (see Glossary). The first *Superintendent of Public Instruction*, W. H. Ruffner, was appointed in 1870. Throughout his tenure, Ruffner struggled against the diversion of funds from the Literary Fund and the virtual absence of state funds for the newly-mandated system of public schools. Nevertheless, he successfully appointed some 1,400 county superintendents and trustees (school board members) and convinced them to start their schools without any state money and without them knowing how much income would be produced from the recently-imposed taxes.[44] Throughout the years following the Civil War, there was constant debate concerning whether or how African-American children should be educated, ultimately resulting in a state-legislated parallel system of public schools in 1870.[45] Neither white nor the African-American public schools were funded adequately, but the conditions and services provided black children were appalling indeed. Nevertheless, state expenditures for public schools rose to approximately $360,000 by 1871 and were nearly matched with local expenditures of $330,000. By 1900, state expenditures slightly exceeded $1 million and again were nearly matched by the localities.[46]

Twentieth Century

In 1902, a rewritten constitution was ratified although the General Assembly did not change the education clause of the Underwood Constitution,

> Free schools to be maintained. The General Assembly shall establish and maintain an efficient system of public free schools throughout the state.[47]

---

[42] *Constitution of Virginia, (1869),* Article VIII, §§1-12.

[43] Virginia did not have the means to adjust assessed values to true market values until 1950 when the first assessment/sales ratio study was conducted by the Department of Taxation.

[44] Virginia Superintendent of Public Instruction, *Annual Report of the State Superintendent of Public Instruction for the Year Ending August 31, 1871.* (Richmond, Virginia: State Superintendent of Public Instruction) at 4.

[45] *Acts of Virginia Assembly of the Commonwealth of Virginia*, 1870.

[46] Heatwole, *Supra* at 245.

[47] *Constitution of Virginia, (1902),* Article IX.

The 1902 Constitution retained the state funding requirement that designated the yield of statewide property tax for public schools but changed the census count used to distribute state aid from 5-21 to 7-20 years of age. It also reinforced previously-enacted state legislation that mandated racially segregated schools with the clause, "White and colored children shall not be taught in the same school."[48]

Four years later in 1906, the Virginia Literary Fund was converted to a school capital construction loan fund.[49] State appropriations for public schools continued to grow during the early years of the twentieth century, although the increased state aid failed to keep pace with population growth. By 1918, the Virginia Education Commission reported that state aid to public schools had exceeded slightly $3.2 million[50] but was still woefully inadequate, providing only one-third the needed resources.[51] In addition to the problems presented by the diversion of funds from the Literary Fund, inadequate state fiscal support became more apparent during the early years of the twentieth century. This problem was created by the extensive variance in the fiscal abilities of localities to support governmental services, including their ability to fund public free schools, a constitutional requirement. Another problem was the inequity created by racial and ethnic barriers. This combination of problems has continued to haunt the Commonwealth throughout the twentieth and into the twenty-first century. Gradually, and often reluctantly, the General Assembly developed a statewide system of public schools and increased state appropriations.

A minimum foundation program structure,[52] entitled the *Basic State School Fund*, was developed, although primary fiscal responsibility was placed upon the localities.[53] The minimum foundation program was popularized nationally during the 1930s, 1940s and 1950s and remains today the dominant structure for funding public schools. The primary purpose of the minimum foundation program is to provide a basic education program throughout a state through use of a fiscal equalization formula,[54] while permitting the generation of additional funds through local taxation. A rather simple minimum foundation program, coupled with a series of categorical flat grants for special education, pupil transportation, vocational education, etc. was institutionalized in Virginia, but it failed to remedy fully the fiscal and educational disparities that existed among local school districts. The disparities were created by a combination of factors, including an inadequate foundation base, variances in local fiscal capacity and tax effort, and, particularly, the parallel system of public schools that provided fewer resources for African-American children.

---

[48] *Ibid.*, §140.

[49] The Literary Fund was popularly known then as the *Williams Building Act* and was passed by the General Assembly, March 15, 1906.

[50] This amount does not include the funds loaned to the localities for school construction projects.

[51] Virginia Education Commission, *Virginia Public Schools, A Survey of a Southern State Public School System.* (New York: World Book Company, 1920), p. 34.

[52] Often referred to as the Strayer-Haig equalization program named for its authors and proponents, Professors George Strayer and Robert Haig, Teachers College, Columbia University, New York.

[53] The percentage of fiscal resources provided by the state does not directly address either the fiscal adequacy or equity goals of a state system of school finance. However, it has proven difficult to achieve either goal for those states that provide a low percentage of state aid for public schools.

[54] A fiscal equalization program in its simplest form establishes a base program cost for each locality, determined by the state, from which a local required tax effort is deducted. The difference, which allocates greater amounts of state aid per-pupil to the less fiscally able localities, is then allocated to each locality, resulting in some movement toward the equalization of educational resources throughout the state.

The 1954 U.S. Supreme Court ruling in *Brown v. Board of Education*[55] and subsequent litigation relating to the desegregation of public schools abolished *de jure* parallel schools systems,[56] but the disparities created by the other factors remained.

As shown in **Table 3**, the percentage of state revenue for public schools had stabilized at approximately 25 percent by the 1920s and then increased to approximately 35 percent by the 1940s, a percentage of support that has remained remarkably constant thereafter. In 1966, for the first time, Virginia passed a general retail sales tax and set the rate at $0.03 per $100 with one-third, or $0.01 of the yield designated for public schools. The other two-thirds of the tax were placed in the state general fund. Another $0.01 was granted to the local governing bodies as an option, an alternative local revenue source subsequently adopted by all counties and municipalities.[57] Initially, the designated $0.01 yield from the state sales tax was allocated to the local school districts based upon each district's proportion of the total school age population and was independent of the Basic State School Fund apportionment. Although the designated sales tax is entitled, *State Sales Tax*, and meets the criterion of a state grant to localities,[58] pursuant to the *Code of Virginia*, the revenue is . . . *considered as funds raised from local sources.*[59] This apparent contradiction between the title of the designated sales tax and state legislation has resulted in inconsistent statistical reports that show significant fluctuation in the amounts of public school revenue and expenditure reported for different fiscal years by state and local education agencies. The reason for Virginia's deviation from accepted accounting rules is that a portion of *Federal Impact Aid*[60] is determined upon the basis of local current expenditures generated by eligible school districts. Since the dedicated sales tax revenue is classified as local revenue, the recipient school districts are entitled to increased federal impact aid.[61]

Despite the introduction of sales tax receipts as a funding source, various education interest groups began to express their displeasure concerning the reluctance of both executive and legislative branches of state government to address effectively the funding disparities among local school districts. In 1968, a lawsuit[62] was filed in the Federal Court of the Western District of Virginia claiming the funding of schools in Virginia violated the Equal Protection Clause of the Fourteenth Amendment of the U.S. Constitution. The plaintiffs alleged the state system of school finance failed to address adequately the educational disparities that exist among Virginia localities. The plaintiffs also alleged that the method that relied exclusively upon property valuation to measure

---

[55] *Supra.*
[56] Considerable evidence exists that shows that public schools, due to housing patterns, culture and tradition, remain segregated by race, ethnicity, and social-economic level.
[57] Knapp, John and Bruce Johnson, *Virginia Issues: The Retail Sales Tax.* (Charlottesville, Virginia: Tayloe Murphy Institute, University of Virginia, December, 1981) at 1-2.
[58] According to the Governmental Accounting Standards Board (GASB), the national organization that sets standards for state and local government accounting, a state tax which is apportioned to localities on a formula independent of where the tax was collected is considered a state grant.
[59] *Code of Virginia (1950),* Title 58 §58-441.48 (d). This citation is prior to the re-codification of statutes; the re-codified citation is *Code of Virginia, (1950)* §58.1-638(D).
[60] 20 *United States Code Annotated*, §7703, Subchapter VIII.
[61] In essence, the Commonwealth of Virginia has *gamed* the system used to apportion federal impact aid.
[62] *Burruss v. Wilkerson*, 310 F. Supp. 592 (W.D. Va. 1969) affirmed 397 U.S. 44, 90 S. Ct. 812 (1970).

Table 3: Virginia Public School Expenditures by Source of Revenue, Selected Years, 1920-21 to 2013-14

School Year	State		Local		Federal		Total	
	Amount	%	Amount	%	Amount	%	Amount	%
Historical Data								
1920-21	4,506,588	25.5	13,197,120	74.5	0	00.0	17,703,708	100.0
1930-31	7,018,410	25.5	20,499,547	74.5	0	00.0	27,517,957	100.0
1940-41	9,359,451	33.5	18,562,576	66.5	0	00.0	27,922,027	100.0
1950-51	43,220,779	36.0	74,698,256	62.1	2,292,485	1.9	120,211,520	100.0
1960-61	104,125,514	35.7	167,982,126	57.5	19,948,920	6.8	292,056,560	100.0
1970-71	257,984,303	30.3	496,880,983	58.3	96,944,736	11.1	851,810,02	100.0
1974-75	404,500,276	35.3	608,048,993	53.0	133,795,080	11.7	1,146,344,349	100.0
1978-79	707,679,683[a]	43.4	745,594,683	45.7	711,725,623	10.9	1,630,999,989	100.0
More Recent Data: Reported Using Conventional Accounting[a]								
1982-83	1,104,214,242	44.1	1,218,264,146	48.6	182,955,696	7.3	2,505,434,084	100.0
1986-87	1,700,734,596	47.2	1,686,633,992	46.9	212,429,760	5.9	3,599,798,348	100.0
1990-91	2,243,755,565	44.4	2,518,882,154	49.8	290,993,564	5.8	5,053,631,283	100.0
1994-95	2,590,343,504	44.8	2,837,289,848	49.0	357,348,705	6.2	5,784,982,057	100.0
1998-99	3,398,878,771	46.8	3,441,615,327	47.4	421,987,012	5.8	7,262,481,110	100.0
2002-03	3,915,698,505	41.4	4,886,864,074	51.7	650,989,969	6.9	9,453,552,548	100.0
2006-07	5,616,135,113	44.6	6,114,823,391	48.6	848,290,617	6.7	12,579,249,121	100.0
2007-08	5,758,171,768	43.6	6,591,291,977	49.9	857,330,800	6.5	13,206,794,545	100.0
2008-09	6,103,026,021	44.9	6,608,951,019	48.6	875,879,632	6.4	13,587,856,672	100.0
2009-10	5,442,528,165	40.3	6,608,951,019[b]	48.9	1,460,053,369[c]	10.8	13,511,532,553	100.0
2010-11	5,216,653,838	39.9	6,512,439,602	49.8	1,356,530,556	10.4	13,085,623,996	100.0
2011-12	5,455,600,295	39.7	6,950,958,330	50.6	1,334,437,028	9.7	13,740,995,652	100.0
2012-13	5,878,572,403	37.8	7,159,487,079	46.0	1,312,703,332	8.4	14,350,762,814	100.0
2013-14	5,980,732,864	37.7	7,374,271,692	46.5	1,291,323,608	8.1	14,646,328,163	100.0
More Recent Data: Reported as Mandated by the General Assembly in *Code of Virginia*, §58.1-638 (D)[d]								
1982-83	866,398,010	34.6	1,456,080,378	58.1	182,955,696	7.3	2,505,434,084	100.0
1986-87	1,332,265,288	37.0	2,055,103,300	57.1	212,429,760	5.9	3,599,798,348	100.0
1990-91	1,800,761,870	35.6	2,961,875,849	58.6	290,993,564	5.8	5,053,631,283	100.0
1994-95	2,041,083,742	35.3	3,386,549,610	58.5	357,348,705	6.2	5,784,982,057	100.0
1998-99	2,713,859,595	37.4	4,126,634,503	56.8	421,987,012	5.8	7,262,481,110	100.0
2002-03	3,134,398,349	33.2	5,668,164,230	60.0	650,989,969	6.9	9,453,552,548	100.0
2006-07	4,480,982,743	35.6	7,249,975,761	57.6	848,290,617	6.7	12,579,249,121	100.0
2007-08	4,607,479,400	34.9	7,741,984,345	58.6	857,330,800	6.5	13,206,794,545	100.0
2008-09	5,013,396,165	36.9	7,698,580,875	56.7	875,879,632	6.4	13,587,856,672	100.0
2009-10	4,392,628,165	32.5	7,658,851,019[c]	56.7	1,460,053,369	10.8	13,511,532,553	100.0
2010-11	4,091,526,935	31.3	7,637,566,505	58.4	1,356,530,556	10.4	13,085,623,996	100.0
2011-12	4,284,134,807	31.2	8,122,423,817	59.1	1,334,437,028	9.7	13,740,995,652	100.0
2012-13	4,666,972,403	32.5	8,371,087,079	58.3	1,312,703,332	8.4	14,350,762,814	100.0
2013-14	4,761,032,864	32.5	8,593,971,692	58.7	1,291,323,608	8.1	14,646,328,163	100.0

Sources: Virginia Department of Education, *Superintendents' Annual Report, 1920-21 to 2010-11.* (Richmond, Va.: VDOE, 1921-2011) and Virginia Department of Education, *Calculation Templates, 2011,2012, 2013,2014.* (Richmond, Va.; VDOE, 2011-2014).

[a] State sales tax proceeds are included in state revenue for public education.
[b] Assumes level-funded local revenue.
[c] Includes $365,187,984 federal stimulus revenue plus an additional $218,985,753 federal revenue contained within Basic State Aid.
[d] State sales tax proceeds are included in local revenue for public education.

local fiscal capacity and set the required local tax effort was flawed. Specifically, the plaintiffs alleged that localities had been granted a broad array of local revenue sources,[63] including the optional retail sales tax, but these sources were ignored for determination of local fiscal capacity. At the time of the litigation, the required local tax effort was based solely upon the yield from a tax rate of $0.60 per $100[64] of True Valuation of Real Property and Public Service Corporation Property (TV)[65] in each locality. The federal district court declined to rule the Virginia school finance system unconstitutional and said . . . *the courts have neither the knowledge, nor the means, nor the power to tailor the public money to fit the varying needs of these students throughout the state.*[66] The court also said the state distribution formula was uniform and the problem was the inability of the localities to raise enough local money and dismissed the case. This case was adjudicated 5 years before the Supreme Court overturned the ruling by the Texas federal district court in *Rodriguez v. San Antonio Independent School District No. 1.*[67] The timing of the litigation in both cases could not have been better for critics of the Virginia system of school finance. Virginia was engaged in drafting a new constitution, and despite negative federal court decisions, complaints made by the plaintiffs influenced both the executive and legislative branches of government. With the ratification of a new constitution in 1971, came a mandated and more comprehensive system of public schools entitled, *Standards of Quality (SOQ)*. Included in the new constitution was the following provision for public schools:

> **Public schools of high quality to be maintained**. The General Assembly shall provide for a system of free public elementary and secondary schools for all children of school age throughout the Commonwealth, and shall *seek to* [Italics added] ensure that an educational program of high quality is established and continually maintained.[68]

And, if the timing were good for the critics of the prior system of school finance, particularly for those who wanted increased state funding, the timing was terrible during the constitutional debates due to federal and state complaints that were occurring elsewhere. The California Supreme Court, also in 1971, ruled its state system for funding public schools was unconstitutional due to inherent disparities created partially by the variance in local taxpaying ability, and therefore, violated the Equal Protection Clause of the California constitution.[69] To help protect the Commonwealth from similar litigation, the words, *seek to*, (see also italics above) were inserted by the Virginia General Assembly into the *education clause* of the 1971

---

[63] Unlike most states, Virginia has not granted fiscal independence to local school boards and employs a system where full fiscal control is vested in the county and independent city governing bodies. Local school boards, whether elected or appointed, are required to submit annually their budgets for approval to their respective local governing bodies, a system that often results in considerable acrimony.

[64] The mathematical equivalent of 6 mills on the dollar, the term used in previous legislation.

[65] True valuation for each locality was determined through application of an assessment/sales ratio study (mathematical adjustment based upon the assessed values of selected properties contrasted to their market values as indicated by recent sales) that was conducted by the Virginia Department of Taxation.

[66] *Burruss v. Wilkerson, Supra* at 574.

[67] On appeal, *Rodriguez v. San Antonio Independent School District No. 1*, 337 F. Supp 280 (1971) became *San Antonio Independent School District No. 1 v. Rodriguez*, 411 U.S. 1, 93 S.Ct. 1278, rehearing denied 411 U.S. 959, 93 S.Ct. 1919 (1973).

[68] *Constitution of Virginia (1971)*. Article VIII, §1.

[69] *Serrano v. Priest*, 96 Cal. Rptr. 601, 135 Cal. Rptr. 584, 226 Cal. Rptr. 584 (1971). As modified 18 Cal. Rptr. 728, 537 P.2d 629) Cal. 1976).

Constitution. This action substantially weakened the ability of critics to challenge successfully through litigation the Virginia system of school finance. A major component to the SOQ was the implementation of a new funding formula. The new funding system for public schools included the transfer of several categorical programs into the minimum foundation program, now entitled *Basic State Aid.* Concurrently, a new measure of fiscal capacity, referred to as the *Local Composite Index (LCI),* was developed. The LCI contained a series of algebraic algorithms that mathematically merge a wealth measure, the true value of locally assessed real property and state-assessed public service corporation property, and two economic indicators: personal income[70] and taxable retail sales receipts. The creation of a single index of taxpaying ability was a direct response to the assertion by the *Burruss v. Wilkerson* plaintiffs that sole reliance upon property valuation was an inadequate measure of fiscal capacity.[71] The individual unadjusted school district indices traditionally have ranged from a high of 1.0000 and greater to a low of approximately 0.1400, ostensibly setting the state share at 0.0 percent for the highest fiscal capacity school districts to 86.0 percent for the least fiscally able.[72] *Save-harmless* provisions were enacted to gain the acquiescence of localities that were scheduled to lose state funds. The LCI as employed initially for school year 1974-75, mathematically set state and local shares equally at 50 percent.[73] For calculation purposes only, the state sales tax was deducted from the state-determined cost of Basic State Aid prior to the application of the individual LCIs, which set the funding responsibilities for both the state and each locality. The state sales tax remained a part of the total revenue provided public schools but lowered the total fiscal responsibilities for both the state and localities.[74] The state-calculated cost of Basic State Aid was based upon a fixed number of instructional personnel per 1,000 pupils in average daily membership (ADM) plus support expenditures per-pupil in ADM (roughly a 60/40 instruction/support ratio). Costs that exceeded the required local share of Basic State Aid plus the series of categorical grants were deemed to be discretionary, i.e., subject to local policy, and were the sole fiscal responsibility of the localities. The Basic State Aid per-pupil costs were calculated biennially as a fixed amount for all local school districts, despite considerable variance in educational needs and economic circumstances that existed among localities. The variance in educational needs among local school districts results from serving a different mix of pupils eligible for special

---

[70] Aggregate adjusted gross income as reported on Virginia individual income tax returns ultimately replaced the personal income measure. This change was necessitated because the Bureau of Economic Analysis, United States Department of Commerce, the source of city and county personal income estimates, ceased making estimates for small independent cities; instead, the Bureau produced only combined city-county estimates for small cities and their adjoining counties.

[71] *Burruss, Supra* at 573.

[72] It is technically possible for the LCI to range from a low of 0.0, but that would require such localities to possess no property, and report no adjusted gross income or taxable retail sales. Typically, a handful of localities register LCIs that exceed 1.0, which raises an interesting issue. In several states, localities that exceed certain limits of state aid are required to remit payments generated from local taxes to the state, or in other states, these calculated payments are deducted from other state aid provisions. Such policies are considered *negative state aid* or *recapture provisions.*

[73] Later, the Commonwealth adopted a policy that provides that no school district will employ a LCI greater than 0.8000, thereby truncating the indices so than school districts that have calculated LCIs at or above 0.8000 will receive 20 percent for the calculated costs of the several state aid programs.

[74] The deduction of taxable retail sales receipts prior to application of the LCI reduced the required appropriations for both state and local agencies. From a mathematical perspective, the deduction of taxable retail sales initially functioned equally. That is, 50 percent could be considered state revenue and 50 percent could be considered local revenue. Later, when the fiscal responsibility for the calculated shares shifted, 55 percent should be considered state and 45 percent local revenue.

education services, vocational training, disadvantaged assistance, and gifted and talented programs. The variance in economic circumstances among school districts occur due to geographical isolation, terrain, weather conditions, size of schools, population density, socioeconomic levels, cost of living, and the relative funding priority given public schools by local governing bodies.

Modern Era: (1979-2010)

Almost immediately following implementation of the SOQ system, critics complained that the state was not fully funding its share and began lobbying the General Assembly and the Governor. By the early 1980s, pressure to *fully fund* the Standards of Quality was being placed upon candidates for public office, including those running for governor. One candidate for governor, Charles Robb, during his 1982 campaign, pledged to address the call to fully fund the SOQ. Following his election and subsequent consultation with leaders of the General Assembly, Robb agreed to have the Joint Legislative Audit and Review Commission (JLARC)[75] conduct an analysis of whether the state was meeting its fiscal obligation to fund public schools. Subsequently, two reports were prepared: *JLARC, Part I,*[76] that was released during the Robb administration in 1986 and *JLARC, Part II*[77] released in 1988 during the administration of Robb's successor, Gerald Baliles. Substantial changes were recommended by JLARC and resulted in the implementation of a complex and tedious methodology that calculates the instructional personnel needs based upon accreditation and SOQ requirements upon a school-by-school basis prior to their aggregation into the total costs for the school district. A number of salaries, loosely representing central tendency and referred to as *Prevailing Salaries* were multiplied by the calculated number of instructional personnel per-school district and then aggregated, providing the total instructional costs for each school district. Support costs, mostly derived upon a statewide basis,[78] were added to the instructional costs, and when divided by ADM, provided the total per-pupil costs for *Basic State Aid.* As mentioned previously, per-pupil costs for *Basic State Aid* were determined individually for each local school district,[79] although the variance in costs among the 136 school districts has remained relatively small and can be attributed primarily to the size of the school districts and their individual schools. Although the measures used to determine state and local shares for each state grant could and should be replicated by interested citizens, statewide data are maintained only by the Virginia Department

---

[75]JLARC is a commission established in 1973 and is comprised of members of both houses. It employs a fulltime staff that is charged with the responsibility to evaluate the operation and performance of state agencies and programs.

[76] Joint Legislative Audit and Review Commission, *Funding the Standards of Quality Part I: Assessing SOQ Costs.* (Richmond, Virginia: Commonwealth of Virginia, 1986).
Retrieved from: http://jlarc.state.va.us/reports/Rpt82.pdf.

[77] Joint Legislative Audit and Review Commission, *Funding the Standards of Quality Part II: SOQ Costs and Distribution.* (Richmond, Virginia: Commonwealth of Virginia, 1988).
Retrieved from: http://leg2.state.va.us/dls/h&sdocs.nsf/By+Year/SD251988/$file/SD25_1988.pdf

[78] During the tenure of Governor Tim Kaine, FYs 2006-10, and in order to reduce the funding obligation of public schools by the Commonwealth, a number of support positions contained in Basic State Aid were reduced.

[79] For FY 2015, per-pupil costs for Basic State Aid are projected to vary from $9,528 for Highland County with approximately 250 pupils in ADM, to $5,323 per-pupil for Virginia Beach City which served approximately 70,000 pupils, a difference of $4,205 per-pupil or approximately 44 percent. However, if several smaller localities are excluded from the comparison, Grayson County with approximately 1,700 pupils in ADM has a projected State Basic Aid per-pupil cost of $6,482, a difference of $3,046, or approximately 18 percent.

of Education. The unavailability of data for other than the major aid programs prevents individuals and organizations from monitoring the calculation of the total package of state aid to the public schools. Thus, the normal checks and balances are not possible. JLARC recommended only minor state revenue increases in its first report, but the cost methodology that followed in its second report resulted in a substantially changed system of school finance which was then coupled with modest increases in state allocations.

L -Estimator

In order to control costs of public schools and reduce the funding obligation of the Commonwealth, JLARC employed a controversial statistic, *the Linear Estimator,* later renamed the *Linear Weighted Average*, and in some instances, the *Linear Estimator* or *Linear Weighted Average* is referred to as the *L-Estimator*.[80] Regardless of the name used, the statistical methodology has remained unchanged, and for the purpose of consistency, the term, *L-Estimator,* is used throughout the remaining chapters of this manual. The *L-Estimator* is a statistic designed to reduce the influence of outliers in the conduct of survey research and was not designed for data sets derived from the total population. Nevertheless, Governor Baliles and the General Assembly followed the recommendation of JLARC to employ the *L-Estimator* for the determination of state aid and local required costs. Use of the *L-Estimator* statistic acts as a restriction on the costs to be shared between the Commonwealth and the localities as follows:

- Average instructional salaries by position for each school district are sorted and ranked into ten sectors,
- Each school district pursuant to its sector is then weighted;
- The greatest weight is applied to the school districts nearest the median salary of the 136 school districts;
- The smallest weight is applied to the school districts that have the highest and lowest mean salaries; and
- *Prevailing salaries* are calculated based upon the applied weights.

The use of the *L-Estimator* has reduced substantially the mathematical influence of localities that possess higher taxpaying ability, pay higher salaries, and employ larger numbers of personnel. A more thorough discussion of the *L-Estimator* is presented in Chapter 3.

As noted in **Table 3**, despite full implementation of the new funding system by 1978-79, the percentage of state revenue for the current operation of public schools (when the revenue receipts from the dedicated taxable retail sales tax are excluded pursuant to the *Code of Virginia,* §58.1-638 (D)) has remained primarily in the low- to mid-30s. The highest percentage of state aid in recent years, 1982-83 to 2013-14, was registered for 1998-99 at 37.4 percent but fell to 32.5 percent for 2009-10, the lowest percentage of state aid for public schools since 1970-71. Since 2009-10, the state percentages have fallen even further. For 2010-11 and 2011-12,[81] the state percentages declined to 31.3 and 31.2, respectively. The state percentages are projected to increase slightly to 32.5 percent for 2012-13 and 2013-14. Although federal revenue receipts comprised nearly 11 percent of total revenue for public schools in 1978-79, the federal share

---

[80] See an early *PowerPoint* presentation by Dickey, Kent C., *Overview of Standards of Quality Funding Process.* Presented to the Standing Committee of the Standards of Quality. (Richmond, Va.: VDOE, 2009).
[81] Estimated for SY 2011-12.

Table 5: Virginia Public School Expenditures Per-pupil in Constant Dollars (2010), by Source of Revenue, Selected Years, 1998-99 to 2012-13

School Year	State	Local	Federal	Total
Data Reported Using Conventional Accounting				
1998-99	$3,996	$4,046	$496	$8,538
2002-03	4,019	5,015	669	9,702
2006-07	4,969	5,410	751	11,131
2007-08	4,874	5,579	715	11,178
2008-09	5,165	5,594	741	11,501
2009-10	4,515	5,483	1,211	11,209
2010-11	4,171	5,207	1,085	10,463
2011-12	4,136	5,270	1,011	10,418
2012-13	$4,500	$5,481	$1,005	$10,987
Data Reported as Mandated by the General Assembly §58.1-638 (D)				
1998-99	$3,191	$4,851	$496	$8,538
2002-03	3,216	5,818	669	9,702
2006-07	3,965	6,415	751	11,131
2007-08	3,900	6,553	715	11,178
2008-09	4,243	6,516	741	11,501
2009-10	3,644	6,354	1,211	11,209
2010-11	3,272	6,106	1,085	10,463
2011-12	3,248	6,158	1,011	10,418
2012-13	$3,573	$6,409	$1,005	$10,987

Source: Virginia Department of Education, *Superintendents' Annual Report, 1998-99 to 2010-11*. (Richmond, Virginia: VDOE, 1999-2011), Virginia Department of Education, *Calculation Templates, 2010-2014*. (Richmond, Virginia: School Finance Calculation Templates, 2010-2014), and United States Department of Labor, *CPI Calculator*. Retrieved from: http://data.bls.gov/cgi-bin/cpicalc.pl.

Virginia Fiscal Effort

As shown in **Table 6**, Virginia's fiscal effort as measured by state and local government revenue for public schools as a percent of personal income[94] rarely has been noteworthy. For school year 1978-89, twenty-five years ago, Virginia generated $44 per $1,000 personal income and achieved a national ranking of 30th. The fiscal effort for school year 2009-10, the most recent year available not based upon estimates, was $42 per $1,000 personal income, and Virginia's national ranking was 35th among 50 states.[95] Based upon National Education Association (NEA) estimates of state and local revenues and personal income data obtained from the Bureau of Economic Analysis, Virginia's effort declined precipitously to $37 per $1,000 of personal income in 2010-11, although its rank among states increased to 34th. Since this decline, the fiscal effort made by Virginia has stabilized at $37 per $1,000 of personal income and remained unchanged for 2011-12 and 2012-13. The $37 per $1,000 personal income generated by the Commonwealth resulted in upward moves to ranks of 33rd and 29th for 2011-12 and 2012-13, respectively. Apparently, other states reduced funds for their public schools even more dramatically than Virginia. From SYs 2003-04 to 2006-07, state revenues for public schools increased by 43 percent, which was partially due to the effect of the Warner-Chichester alliance discussed earlier. The growth in state revenues continued from SYs 2007-08 to 2008-09. From SYs 2003-04 to 2008-09, the growth in state revenues for the Commonwealth increased by 37.6 percent. During the same time period, the nation increased state appropriations by a more modest 24.0 percent. Virginia's spike in state revenues resulted in a statistical increase in fiscal effort, as measured by state and local revenue for public schools per $1,000 personal income and a substantial rise in the national ranking for the Commonwealth. Since FY 2008-09, the lack of growth in state revenue for public schools has reduced the fiscal effort generated by the Commonwealth. From 2008-09 to 2012-13, state appropriations for public schools fell by over 5 percent, while the nation continued to increase state revenues, albeit at a reduced rate of less than 2 percent.

Current Fiscal Crisis

Evidence abounds that shows Virginia, like nearly all other states and the nation as a whole, has suffered a recession exceeded only by the *Great Depression* of the 1930s. An excellent analysis by James Regimbal[96] indicated the fiscal problems faced by both state and local governments will continue for several years and likely will become even more difficult. The easy budget reductions have already been made by both state and local governments.[97] Traditionally, local superintendents and their school boards, when faced with budget reductions, attempt to protect their instructional programs, particularly programs where they are held accountable by the state and the public. Typical of the strategies that are being used by local school districts include:

---

[94] Virginia is a relatively high income state. In CY 2009 the state's per capita was 112 percent of the U.S. average and the state ranked 7th among the 50 states. Because of its high income the state's fiscal effort ranks much lower in relation to personal income than it does using some other measure such as spending per-pupil. Source of income data: Bureau of Economic Analysis, "State Personal Income 2009." News release dated March 25, 2010. Retrieved from: http://www.bea.gov/newsreleases/regional/spi/sqpi_newsrelease.htm

[95] National Education Association, *Rankings of States and Estimates of School Statistics, 2011-13*). (Washington, D.C.: NEA, 2011-2013).

[96] Regimbal, Jr., James J., "Virginia's State Budget – A Train Wreck About to Happen," (Charlottesville, Virginia: *The Virginia News Letter*, Weldon-Cooper Center For Public Service, Vol. 85: No. 5, October, 2009) at pp. 1-9.

[97] *Ibid.* at p. 1.

Table 6: Virginia State and Local Government Revenue for Public Schools Per $1,000 Personal Income, Selected Years, 1978-79 to 2012-13

School Year	Revenue Per $1,000 Personal Income	Rank Among States
Actual		
1978-79	$44	30
1982-83	36	43
1986-87	38	35
1990-91	40	38
1994-95	37	40
1998-99	39	35
2002-03	39	37
2006-07	42	22
2007-08	45	31
2008-09	45	38
2009-10	42	35
Estimates		
2010-11[a]	37	34
2011-12[a]	37	33
2012-13[a]	$37	29

Source: School Years 1978-79 to 2009-10 provided by National Education Association, *Rankings of the States, 1978-79 to 2009-10.* (Washington, D.C.: NEA, 1979 to 2011). Retrieved from: http://www.nea.org/assets/img/content/NEA_Rankings_And_Estimates-2013_(2).pdf

[a] Calculated by authors from data drawn from National Education Association, *Estimates of School Statistics, 2011, 2012 and 2013.* (Washington, D.C.: NEA, 2011-2013) and Bureau of Economic Analysis, *Personal Income by State, 2011 to 2013.* (Washington, D.C.: United States Department of Commerce, 2011-2014).

- Reduction in the number of personnel, including classroom teachers, thereby raising pupil/teacher ratios. Normally, the increased pupil/teacher ratios are achieved through retirement of personnel and non-renewal of probationary teachers, although in some instances, tenured teachers are terminated;
- Early retirement incentives are provided senior personnel and their replacements are made from either existing personnel or less experienced and credentialed personnel;
- Reduction and/or elimination of administrative, instructional and support personnel not required by the SOQ;
- Freezing salaries (in some instances step increases are retained, but in other instances, steps also are frozen);
- Reduction in extra pay for extra duties, e.g., stipends for coaching, band directing, etc.;
- Implementation of joint service agreements between school districts, their local governing bodies, and among other school districts. Such agreements are usually accompanied with the introduction of centralized policy boards;
- Merger of schools, commonly with the closure of older buildings and those facilities that have high energy consumption and/or have exhibited an unacceptable record of maintenance costs;
- Consolidation of administrative and support facilities;
- Elimination of rental and service agreements;
- Reduction and/or elimination of non-SOL programs, including reduction in tuition grants for pupils served by Governors' Schools, reduced resources for gifted and talented programs and similar enrichment activities;
- Deferral of maintenance projects and equipment; and
- Extension of the longevity of motor vehicles, including postponement of scheduled school bus purchases.

Observations

A substantial part of the current crisis is due to the fiscal decisions made by previous administrations, General Assemblies, and many local governing bodies. It is unfortunate that long-term tax policies often have been established, i.e. reduction and/or elimination of unpopular taxes,[98] during highly-energized national, state, and local economies that inevitably force reexamination of policy during the most difficult times. The most obvious example is the so-called *Car-Tax* relief that biennially forces the transfer of $1.9 billion state revenue to the localities. The transfer of these replacement revenues from the state to the localities should be phased-out, perhaps over two or more biennia. Under current fiscal conditions, this would be a painful political process, both for the state and the localities. It is also unfortunate that when the Commonwealth substantially increased state funds for public schools for FY 2005, most localities either decreased or level-funded their local appropriations for public schools.[99] If the localities had followed this seldom-seen lead of the state, fiscal disparities among local school districts would have been reduced, and the recent budget reductions would not have been as devastating to the public schools. On the other hand, it is fortunate that Virginia has the potential, without the need to make extraordinary fiscal effort, to remedy the current fiscal plight

---

[98] The authors recognize that taxes are rarely popular.

[99] *Supra.*, Driscoll and Salmon.

confronting public schools and other governmental agencies. The state budget reductions for public schools have affected negatively the quality of public schools throughout the Commonwealth and especially in the lower fiscal-capacity school districts. Not all of the local responses to budget reductions have been harmful, and in some instances likely have increased cost efficiency without affecting educational quality. However, freezing personnel salaries for several years will inevitably prove harmful to public schools. Although reductions have been determined through use of the LCI, the equalization component of the state formulae, the lower fiscal-capacity school districts have suffered the most. Since the lower-fiscal-capacity school districts depend primarily upon state aid to fund their budgets, reductions in state aid inevitably result in larger total budget reductions for the lower-fiscal-capacity school districts.

Past governors and general assemblies have relied nearly exclusively upon cost containment and have implemented massive budget reductions for virtually all state agencies in order to balance state budgets. The reductions have fallen particularly hard upon public education, both higher education and elementary and secondary schools. Both have attempted to convince the public that their constitutional obligation to provide and maintain a high quality system of public schools has been fulfilled by engaging in a series of charades. These charades include use of federal stimulus funds to fund *Basic State Aid* and reductions in the caps for the number of support personnel to lower the number of support personnel and costs required to fund the SOQ. History continues to repeat itself as funds have been stripped once again from the 200-year-old *Literary Fund*. Hopefully, with the election of a new governor, a more progressive approach will be taken regarding the funding of public education.

Chapter 3

Source of Funds for Public Education
in the Commonwealth of Virginia

Public schools in the Commonwealth of Virginia are financed by revenue derived from four sources, **local**, **state** plus revenue received from the **dedicated 1¢ state sales tax**,[100] and **federal** agencies. Contained in **Table 7** are the total revenue/expenditure and percent of total, by source, for FY 2012. The Commonwealth contributed 34.0% of total revenue/expenditure for public schools in FY 2002, the state 1¢ dedicated sales tax provided 8.6%, the localities appropriated 50.8%, and the federal government contributed 6.6%. The trend since FY 2002 is presented in **Table 8.**

Budget Approval for School Purposes

Pursuant to §15.2-2503, all officers and heads of departments, offices, districts, boards, commissions, and agencies of every locality shall, on or before the first day of April of each year, prepare and submit to the governing body an estimate of the amount of money needed during the ensuring fiscal year for his department, office, district, board, commission or agency.

In accordance to §22.1-93, the governing body of counties are required to prepare and approve an annual budget for educational purposes by **May first or within thirty days of the receipt by the county of estimates of state funds**, whichever shall later occur, and governing body of a municipality shall prepare and approve an annual budget for educational purposes by **May fifteen or within thirty days of receipt . . . of the estimates of state funds.** (Bold added) The governing body shall prepare and approve a budget for informative and fiscal planning purposes only, containing a complete itemized and classified plan of all contemplated expenditures and all estimated revenues and borrowings for the locality for the ensuing fiscal year. The governing body shall approve the budget and fix a tax rate for the budget year no later than the date on which the fiscal year begins [July 1]. The governing body shall annually publish the approved budget on the locality's website, if any, or shall otherwise make the approved budget available in hard copy as needed to citizens for inspection.

The Superintendent of Public Instruction shall, no later than the fifteenth day following final adjournment of the Virginia General Assembly in each session, submit estimates to be used for budgetary purposes relative to the Basic School Aid Formula to each school district and to the local governing body of each county, city and town that operates a separate school district. Such estimates shall be for each year of the next biennium or for the then next fiscal year.

---

[100] The dedicated 1¢ state sales tax is, by definition, revenue derived from state resources; however, pursuant to the Code of Virginia, §58.1-638(D), revenue received from the 1¢ state sales tax is considered local revenue.

Table 7

Revenue/Expenditure by Source for the Commonwealth
of Virginia, FY 2012

Source	Revenue/Expenditure	Percent
Local	$6,950,958,330	50.6
State	4,284,134,807	31.2
State 1¢ Dedicated Sales Tax	1,171,465,488	8.5
Federal	1,334,437,028	9.7
Total	$13,740,995,652	100.0

Source: Virginia Department of Education, *Superintendent's Annual Report, Table 15.* (Richmond, Virginia: VDOE, 2013).

Table 8

Percent Revenue/Expenditure by Source for the
Commonwealth of Virginia, Selected Fiscal Years, 2002 to 2012

Fiscal Year	Local	State	State Sales Tax	Federal	Total
2002	50.8%	34.0%	8.6%	6.6%	100.0%
2004	51.5%	32.7%	8.6%	7.2%	100.0%
2006	50.1%	33.3%	9.5%	7.1%	100.0%
2008	49.9%	34.9%	8.7%	6.5%	100.0%
2010	50.1%	33.3%	9.5%	7.1%	100.0%
2012	50.6%	31.2%	8.5%	9.7%	100.0%

Source: Virginia Department of Education, *Superintendent's Annual Report,* Table 15. (Richmond, Virginia: VDOE, 2013).

Appropriations for Public Schools

The governing bodies city town council have the authority to accept or reduce the estimate of needs request. Pursuant to §22.1-94, a governing body may make appropriations to a school board from the funds derived from local levies and from any other funds available, for operation, capital outlay and debt service in the public schools. Such appropriations shall be not less than the cost apportioned to the governing body for maintaining an educational program meeting the *Standards of Quality (SOQ)* for the several school districts prescribed as provided by law. The **amount appropriated** by the governing body for public schools **shall relate to its total only or to such major classifications** prescribed by the Board of Education pursuant §22.1-115. The appropriation may be made on the same periodic basis as the governing body makes appropriations to other departments and agencies. (Bold added)

System of Accounting; Statements of Funds Available; Classification of Expenditures

Pursuant to §22.1-115,

The State Board, in conjunction with the Auditor of Public Accounts, shall establish and require of each school district a modern system of accounting for all school funds, state and local, and the treasurer or other fiscal agent of each school district shall render each month to the school board a statement of the funds in his hands available for school purposes. The Board shall prescribe the following major classification for expenditures of school funds: (i) instruction, (ii) administration, attendance and health, (iii) pupil transportation, (iv) operation and maintenance, (v) school food services and other non-instructional operations, (vi) facilities, (vii) debt and fund transfers, (viii) technology, and (ix) contingency reserves.

Revenue Sources

- Local Taxes -- The primary revenue source of local revenue for public schools in the Commonwealth is provided by property taxes on real estate and public service corporations. For FY 2013, county governments received 57.6% of their revenue from general property taxes, while the municipalities received 47.0%. Varied other local taxes furnished the remaining funds: 42.4% for county governments and 53.0% for the municipalities. An array of local revenue sources are employed, including the following taxes, optional local sales, personal property, utility, business license, motor vehicle license, hotel and motel room, and restaurant food. There is considerable variance among localities regarding tax yields derived from the available taxes. For example, Bath County received 73.7% of its revenue from property taxes on real and public service corporations, while Covington City derived only 15.3% from the same source.[101]

- State Sales Tax (Dedicated) -- As cited previously, pursuant to §58.1-638(D): . . . the dedicated 1¢ state sales tax is considered local revenue, and the net revenue yield shall be apportioned and distributed among counties and cities upon the basis of the latest yearly estimate of the population of cities and counties ages five to 19, provided by the *Weldon Cooper Center for Public Service* of the University of Virginia. The population count shall include persons who are domiciled in orphanages or charitable institutions, dependents living on military or federal reservations, members of the military under 20 years of age with parents who reside in the local school district, individuals in state hospitals, state training centers, mental health facilities, persons incarcerated, and persons attending institutions of higher education where their parents legally reside.

- State Taxes -- Despite the harsh economic climate, particularly during the Biennia 2011, 2012 and 2013, 2014, due to its wealth and economic capacity, Virginia has the potential to remedy the current fiscal plight facing public schools. According to the *Bureau of Economic Analysis*, U.S. Department of Commerce, Virginia ranked 8th in per capita

---

[101] Virginia Auditor of Public Accounts, *Comparative Cost Report, (Draft 2013)*. (Richmond, Virginia: Commonwealth of Virginia, 2013).

personal income among the fifty states in CY 2012,[102] but ranked among the lowest in the nation for its fiscal effort to fund public schools. There are severe funding disparities among Virginia school districts, with the least affluent localities suffering the most. Solving education funding problems will not be easy, but if economic crises have a saving grace, it is in forcing stakeholders to look for the most efficient ways to operate. Several biennia ago, during a sustained period of rapid economic growth, a number of ill-advised tax reductions were legislated. The state may well have to reconsider the tax abatements[103] and increase taxes if public education is to be maintained even at its current most basic level. The most egregious tax abatement fiasco was the so-called reduction of the *Car Tax,* a centerpiece of the campaign and tenure of Governor Jim Gilmore (R). Gilmore promised the electorate that if elected, he would introduce legislation to eliminate the motor vehicle tax. However, once Gilmore was elected, it became clear that it would require a change to the Virginia Constitution in order to rescind taxes on motor vehicles, one of several items classified as personal property taxes. The 1971 Virginia Constitution *segregated* personal property taxes, including motor vehicle taxes, so that all forms of personal property taxes can only be taxed by local governments.

- Amending the Virginia Constitution is a difficult task under any circumstance, particularly so during the one four-year tenure as governor. As an alternative and in order to fulfill his promise to the public, Governor Gilmore introduced legislation (Personal Property Tax Relief Act of 1998, or PPTRA), subsequently approved by the General Assembly, to transfer state general fund revenue to localities that agreed to reduce their motor vehicle taxes relative to the state transfer.[104] The intention of Governor Gilmore was for the Commonwealth to ultimately replace with state revenue, raised incrementally over several biennia, the total lost yield of the motor vehicle tax, heretofore the prerogative of the localities, a goal never achieved. The General Assembly has continued to struggle to transfer state revenue to localities in order to honor the promise made by Gilmore to rescind the *Car Tax.* Ultimately, the annual transfer of state funds to honor the promise made by Gilmore was capped at $950 million per fiscal year. For the Biennium 2015, 2016, the state transfer of revenue to replace the motor vehicle tax of the localities is projected to be $1.9 billion. Thus, the transfer state revenue imposed by PPTRA is projected to reduce the state general fund by $950 million annually, or approximately 5.7% of total general fund revenue.

---

[102] Bureau of Economic Analysis, *Survey of Current Business.* (Washington, D.C.: United States Department of Commerce, 2013). Retrieved from: http://www.bea.gov/newsreleases/regional/spi/2013/spi0313.htm.

[103] See for example, Virginia Economic Development Partnership. *Business Incentives-Investing in Each Other.* (Richmond, Va.: VEDP, 2014). Retrieved from: http://yesvirginia.org/ProBusiness/BusinessIncentives.

[104] *Personal Property Tax Relief Act (PPTRA of 1998),* consisted of §§ 58.1-3523 et. seq.

CHAPTER 4

The Commonwealth of Virginia Formulae for Funding Public Elementary and Secondary Education

State aid to Public Schools is provided through the *Direct Aid to Public Education* through annual appropriations contained in the Appropriation Acts. The General Assembly is responsible for making the appropriations while the Superintendent of Public Instruction[105] with the support of the Virginia Department of Education (VDOE) administers the funds. Contained below is a summary of Direct Aid appropriations made by the 2013 General Assembly.[106]

Fund (Appropriations)	FY 2014
▪ General Funds (Including 1.125¢ of the dedicated state sales tax)	$5.3 billion
▪ Trust and Agency Funds	598.4 million
▪ Special Funds	3.0 million
▪ Federal Funds	870.9 million
Total	$6.8 billion

Appropriations contained within General Funds, Trust and Agency Funds, and Special Funds are funded from state resources. The above appropriations are distributed by the VDOE through no less than 51 separate funds. The projected allocations, by fund, for FYs 2013 and 2014 are available at the VDOE website.[107] The funding formulae, by fund, also are available at the same website. Most of the federal funds, while obtained from federal agencies, are administered by the Virginia Department of Education (VDOE), and some are referred to as *flow-through allocations*. A few federal appropriations, e.g., *P.L. 974 Federal Impact Aid*,[108] are allocated directly to qualifying school districts by the Bureau of Impact Aid, United States Department of Education.

Pursuant to the *Virginia Constitution, Article VIII, §2 the Standards of Quality (SOQ)* for the several school districts shall be determined and prescribed from time to time by the Board of Education, subject to revision only by the General Assembly.

> The General Assembly shall determine the manner in which funds are to be provided for the cost of maintaining an educational program meeting the prescribed SOQ, and shall provide for the apportionment of the cost of such program between the Commonwealth and the local units of government comprising such school districts. Each unit of local government shall provide its portion of such cost by local taxes or from other available funds.

---

[105] *Constitution of Virginia*, Article VIII, §6. Superintendent of Public Instruction, *Code of Virginia*, §22.1-23. Duties in general, and 8 VAC 20-510-10 (7).

[106] *Chapter 806*, 2013 General Assembly.

[107] See: http://www.doe.virginia.gov/school_finance/budget/calc_tools/index.shtml

[108] Title VIII, §§8002, 8003, and 8007 of the *Elementary and Secondary Education Act of 1965* (ESEA)), and the program's regulations 34 CFR §222. (Commonly referred to as P.L. 874 and 815).

This section of the Virginia Constitution is written so that *unless the General Assembly takes action* (Italics added) to revise the SOQ adopted by the Virginia Board of Education, the adopted standards become law. Relative to the structure of government in most other states, the State Board of Education possesses greater authority and influence regarding the governance of public elementary and secondary education.

The specific requirements of the SOQ, including required programs, services, and staffing are contained in *Code of Virginia* and the annual appropriations act. Most important, contained in the appropriation acts are the specific funding formulae for allocation of funds for public schools.

The Typical State System of School Finance

The system of school finance employed by Virginia is classified technically as a *Foundation Program* or *Minimum Foundation Program*[109] and conforms generally to a typical state system of school finance that is graphically displayed in **Figure 1**.

Figure 1: Typical Model of a State System of School Finance

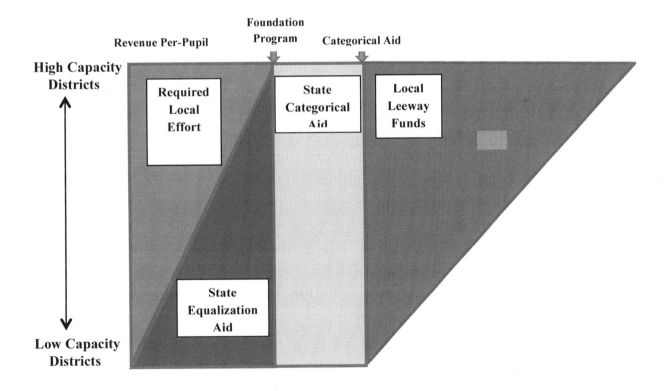

---

[109] First conceived and developed by George Strayer and Robert Haig, Teacher's College, Columbia University during the 1930s.

The *Foundation Program* grant is displayed in blue and red sections, representing the *Required Local Effort (RLE)* and state equalization aid, respectively. The algebraic formula for a Foundation Program is:

$$S_i = P_iF_i - UV_i$$

Where: S_i = State equalization grant to $_i$th district
P_i = Units of the $_i$th district (pupils, teachers, other measures of educational need)
F = Foundation program per unit value (determined by the state)
U = Uniform Required Local Effort (RLE)
V_i = Local fiscal capacity

Where: O_i = Local Leeway (local tax levy x local tax base)

The state equalization and required local effort portions of the foundation program are normally allocated as general aid, permitting the school district to expend both state and local revenue for any legal purpose. Nationally, the most common measure of school districts' ability to pay is real property, i.e. Equalized (True) Valuation of real property. However, several states, including the Commonwealth of Virginia use a combination of several measures.[110] The yellow section represents state categorical aid, often allocated through a series of flat grants. The algebraic formula for a Flat Grant Program is:

$$S_i = P_iF$$

Where: S_i = State flat grant to $_i$th district
P_i = Units of the $_i$th district (pupils, teachers, other measures of educational need)
F = Flat grant unit value

Categorical aid is appropriated for specific programs and purposes, including special education, vocational education, gifted and talented education, and others. Often contained within the language of the appropriation is a requirement that the local school district expend the revenue for the designated programs and purposes. The green section represents the local leeway funds, i.e., local discretionary allocations, and is normally a feature of a foundation program formula. Local leeway revenue, like foundation aid, can be expended for any legal purpose. Note that the foundation program is not designed to *eliminate* but to *reduce* per-pupil disparities among local school districts. Instead, the foundation program is primarily designed to provide a minimum level of educational programs and services. The existence of a local leeway component within a foundation program normally is the result of the high wealth districts demanding the right to provide higher quality educational services than the low wealth districts. Justification for this feature within a foundation program was provided by *Lighthouse language*. That is, if the high wealth areas are permitted to out-spend their neighbors, their districts will act as beacons of light and encourage other districts to follow their example. The problem, of course, is that the low

---

[110] Virginia employs an index of fiscal capacity, the Local Composite Index (LCI). Further discussion of the LCI is presented in the section, **Determination of the Fiscal Capacities of Local School Districts**.

wealth districts lack the necessary fiscal resources without exerting extraordinary fiscal effort to match the educational programs and services provided by the high wealth districts. Inevitably, the larger the dependency on local leeway funds, the greater is the level of disparate funding among school districts. Thus, two questions arise: Does the state permit excessive per-pupil disparities so that the high wealth districts may provide quality educational programs and services while the low wealth districts offer only meager programs? Or, does the state restrict the generation of local leeway funds, often resulting in inadequate programs for all districts?

The Commonwealth of Virginia System of School Finance

Displayed in **Figure 2** is a graphical representation of the Commonwealth of Virginia System of School Finance. Notice that the Foundation Program (State Basic Aid), displayed in blue, white, red, while pink represents the Required Local Effort (RLE), including the 1¢ dedicated state sales tax (RLE), Federal Revenue Deduction,[111] and the State Equalization Aid (SEA). Categorical Aid,[112] displayed in yellow, also has a LRE in order to qualify for SEA, shown in red. Note also that the dedicated 1¢ state sales tax is deducted before state and local shares are determined, thereby permitting the state sales tax to be simultaneously used as part to the local school districts' required effort while reducing the obligation of the Commonwealth to fund State Basic Aid. Unlike most states, Virginia allocates state categorical aid through an equalization formula, i.e. Local Composite Index (LCI). The employment of LCI to allocate state categorical aid does reduce funding disparities among local school districts; however, since the percent of total revenue provided from state sources is low relative to other states, the localities are forced to bear primary responsibility for funding public schools and excessive per-pupil disparities are the predictable result.[113] Approximately 80 percent of the states, including Virginia, rely on the venerable foundation program formula to distribute state revenue to the public schools; however, there is considerable variance among the 50 states regarding the methodology used to determine and distribute state revenue. All states, including Virginia, that employ an equalization formula, e.g. Foundation Program or Minimum Foundation Program, require that they answer the following two questions: (1) How does the Commonwealth determine the shared costs of public schooling and (2) How does the Commonwealth distribute state revenue[114] and establish local funding responsibilities.

---

[111]The Commonwealth makes a technical adjustment, referred to as *Federal Revenue Deduction* that reduces the state obligation to fund *State Basic Aid*. The so-called Technical Adjustment is likely illegal, as was the procedure used earlier when the state briefly deducted *Federal Impact Aid* during the 1960s. See: Shepheard v. Godwin, 280 F.Supp.869 (VA., 1968). See also: Burnette, Mark A., *The Evolution of the Non-supplant Issue in the Federal Funding of Public Education: The Policy in Virginia and its National Implications*. Unpublished Ed.D. (Blacksburg, VA.: Virginia Polytechnic Institute and State University, 2005).

[112] Categorical aid is any grant that requires the expenditure of funds for certain designated programs or purposes. Virginia employs four classes of categorical programs, *SOQ Grants Other than State Basic Aid, Incentive Aid, Lottery-Funded Grants, and Categorical Aid*; pursuant to the language of school finance, technically, all four types are different forms of categorical aid programs.

[113]See: Baker, Bruce D, David G. Sciarra and Danielle Farrie, *Is School Funding Fair? A National Report Card*, 3rd Ed. (Newark, N.J.: Education Law Center, Rutgers University, 2014).

[114] Technically referred to as the *Intergovernmental Transfer of Revenue.*

Figure 2: Commonwealth of Virginia Model of School Finance

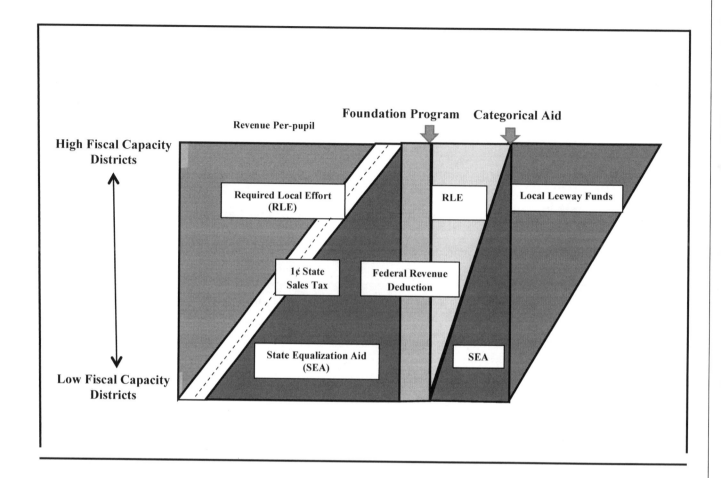

Determination for the Standards of Quality Costs (SOQ) of Public Schools

As discussed earlier, the Virginia Constitution is obligated, as a minimum, to fund the **Standards of Quality (SOQ)**.[115] Contained within the SOQ are the following 11 separate funds and the FY 2014 appropriations:[116]

Fund	2014 Appropriation
▪ State Basic Aid;	$2,351,412,945
▪ One ¢ Dedicated State Sales Tax;	1,218,700,000
▪ Textbooks (Split-funded);	*Lottery Funded*
▪ Vocational Education;	53,873,016
▪ Gifted Education;	32,299,221
▪ Special Education;	367,217,196
▪ Prevention, Intervention & Remediation	85,370,938

---

[115] *Constitution of Virginia (1971),* Article VIII, §1.
[116] See Appendix A for funding formulae.

- VRS Retirement;   304,754,993
- Social Security;   182,538,742
- Group Life Insurance; and   11,486,365
- Remedial Summer School (Split-funded).   11,706,326
    Subtotal (SOQ Accounts)   **$5,194,506,961**

SOQ Funding Explanation

- The SOQ was established in the *1971 Constitution of Virginia*[117] as the minimum educational program which must be provided by all school districts;
- The specific requirements of the SOQ are specified in the *Code of Virginia* and the *Annual Appropriation Acts*, including funding formulae, required programs, and minimum staffing ratios;
- The shared costs, i.e. percent responsible between local school districts and the Commonwealth, are calculated through application of the *Local Composite Index (LCI)* for all 136 school districts and are unique to each school district.
- Each fund under the *SOQ*, excluding the *one ¢ Dedicated State Sales Tax*, contains a mandated local match, i.e. *Required Local Effort (RLE)*. The RLE is determined through application of the *Local Composite Index*; and
- Localities are permitted to expend more than their minimum required effort and offer programs and employ staff beyond what is required in the *SOQ*. These additional local funds are discretionary and technically known as *Local Leeway Funds*;
- Three components of SOQ cost are funded:
    1. Required number of instructional positions (Based on SOQ staffing standards contained the *Virginia Code, Annual Appropriations Act, Virginia Board of Education Regulations*, and the funded salaries and fringe benefits rates applied to the several instructional positions);
    2. Recognized support positions (With funded salaries and fringe benefit rates applied); and,
    3. Recognized non-personal support costs (e.g., supplies, utilities, etc.).
- The support cost components (2 and 3) are funded primarily through *State Basic Aid* upon a *prevailing cost*[118] basis, with support positions capped (limited) based on a ratio of support personnel to instructional positions.[119] Funding for most SOQ accounts is provided on a per-pupil basis and distributed based upon March 31st (Current Year) Average Daily Membership (ADM).[120]

- The costs are determined on a school-by-school basis by identifying three variables:
    1. Number of *prevailing instructional positions*;
    2. Number of *prevailing support positions*; and

---

[117] *Constitution of Virginia (1971), Supra.*
[118] The use of the term *prevailing costs* or *prevailing positions* indicates that the number obtained has been derived through use of the *linear estimator* (i.e. linear weighted average).
[119] In order to avoid reinstatement of taxes reduced during high economic growth, the Commonwealth slashed agency resources during the 2010 General Assembly, including the number of support positions heretofore funded from a combination state and local revenue.
[120] Additional explanation regarding this feature of cost determination will be provided during presentation of the fiscal capacity measure, i.e. *Local Composite Index*.

3. *Prevailing salaries*, by position.

1. Number of instructional positions required to comply with the *Code of Virginia*, §22.1-253.13:2. **Standard 2. Instructional, administrative, and support personnel (Examples are presented below).**

Elementary Grades

Ratios:	K	--	24:1	(No more than 29:1 with Teacher Aide)
	1-3	--	24:1	(No more than 30:1)
	4-6	--	25:1	(No more than 35:1)

2. Classroom teachers in the elementary schools are identified through use of *brackets*. For example, kindergarten teachers are identified by brackets of 1-24 pupils in Average Daily Membership without an aide. If the number of pupils exceed 24, either an aide or another teacher is required. Since it is less expensive to employ an aide until the pupils reach 30, this becomes the calculated cost. However, if the number of pupils meet or exceed 30, then two classroom teachers are employed, each serving 15 pupils.

Secondary Grades

3. Classroom teachers assigned to middle and high schools are determined through application of simple student/teacher ratios.

Middle Schools	--	21:1 (Pupils to FTE teaching positions)
High Schools	--	21:1 (Pupils to FTE teaching positions)

4. For both elementary and secondary schools, other instructional personnel, e.g. principals, assistant principals, guidance counselors, librarians, etc. have been identified through application of simple pupil/teacher ratios that are based upon the total number of enrolled FTE pupils in ADM per-school. For example, principals are identified by implementation of the following ratios:

School Type		Pupils		Principal
Elementary Schools	--	1-299	=	½ time Principal
	--	≥300	=	1 fulltime Principal
Middle Schools	--	≥1	=	1 fulltime Principal
High Schools	--	≥1	=	1 fulltime Principal

5. For both elementary and secondary schools, support personnel are generated through simple ratios that are based upon the total number of enrolled FTE pupils in ADM per-school. For example, clerical personnel are identified by implementation of the following ratios:

School Type		Pupils		Principal
Elementary Schools	--	1-299	=	Part time Clerk
	--	≥300	=	1 fulltime Clerk
	--	≥200	=	1 fulltime Clerk + 1 fulltime Clerk per each 600 pupils over 200 pupils
High Schools	--	≥200	=	1 fulltime Clerk + 1 fulltime Clerk per 600 pupils over 200 pupils

6. Prevailing salaries and the required positions are determined, by position, through application of the *Linear Estimator* (*Linear Weighted Average*) statistic.

Explanation of the Linear Estimator (Linear Weighted Average)

The *Linear Estimator (L-Estimator)* is one of several statistics developed to reduce the statistical influence of *Outliers*. According to Hosking,

> The main advantage of L-moments over conventional moments is that L-moments, being linear functions of the data, suffer less from the effects of sampling variability: L-moments are more robust than conventional moments to outliers in the data and enable more secure inferences to be made from small samples about an underlying probability distribution. L-moments sometimes yield more efficient parameter estimates than the maximum likelihood estimates.[121]

Central to this discussion is that the use of the *L-Estimator* to identify prevailing salaries and positions by the Commonwealth is not to reduce the influence of outliers; instead the intent is to understate the salaries of personnel, thereby reducing the fiscal obligation of the Commonwealth. As discussed by Hosking, the *L-Estimator* is intended to be used to reduce the effects created by outliers during the analysis of small sample data returns. There is little justification for employment of an *L-Estimator* when the analysis is applied to the entire population, as is the biennial analysis of the salaries paid instructional personnel in the Commonwealth. There are other statistical measures of central tendency, including the mean and median, which are more appropriate and can be justified.

Displayed in **Chart 1** is a graphic representation of the *L-Estimator* used by the Commonwealth to derive *Prevailing Salaries* and *Prevailing Positions*. As employed by the State, the individual school districts are sorted by the mean salaries[122] paid the various instructional positions, e.g. elementary teachers, secondary teachers, assistant elementary principals, elementary principals,

---

[121] J. R. M. Hosking, J.R.M., "L-Moments: Analysis and Estimation of Distributions Using Linear Combinations of Order Statistics. (*Journal of the Royal Statistical Society. Series B* (Methodological, Vol. 52: No. 1, 1990) at 105-124.
[122] See Appendices D and E for examples of the variance in instructional salaries among local school districts.

Chart 1: Model of L-Estimator with 10 sectors and weights of 1-5

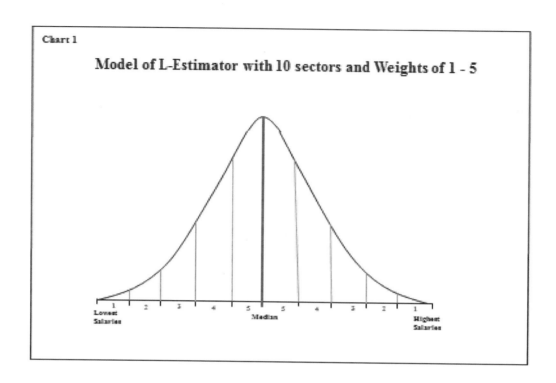

etc. For each instructional position, weights are applied to the mean salaries by school district pursuant to the sector where the school district resides. Specifically, school districts that reside the nearest to the median school district[123] are weighted five, while those school districts that reside in the sector farthest from the median school district are weighted one. The weighted salaries, by instructional position, are aggregated and divided by the numbers of relevant positions, which produces the *prevailing salaries for each instructional position category.* Those school districts, regardless of the numbers of students served or the instructional personnel employed, that reside nearest the median school district have the greatest mathematical influence on the derivation of the *prevailing salaries.* In a perverse manner, the largest school district in the Commonwealth, Fairfax County/Fairfax City Public Schools, which is projected for FY 2014 to serve 179,387.05 students, has no more statistical influence than Northampton County Public Schools that is projected to serve 1,557.10. Fairfax County/Fairfax City students represent 14.6 percent of total students who will be enrolled in the Commonwealth; Northampton County will serve 0.1 percent. For FY 2012, Fairfax County/Fairfax City paid their elementary teachers $62,415.80, fourth highest salary among 132 school districts; concurrently, Northampton County

---

[123] Note that the term *median school district* does not represent median salaries or positions; instead, the term, *median school district*, is used in order to avoid the mathematical influence created by size, as measured by the number of students enrolled. A true *median* would represent the salary or position median, and the size of the school district would influence calculation of *prevailing salaries* or *positions.*

paid its elementary teachers approximately one-half of the Fairfax County/City salary, $34,239.62, the lowest mean salary for elementary teachers in the Commonwealth.

Arrayed in **Chart 2** is the same Model of the *L-Estimator*, plus a curve that displays the approximate numbers of instructional personnel for the same school districts presented in **Chart 1**. It is apparent from a review of this chart, when the numbers of instructional personnel are assigned, by school district, the result is a dramatically skewed bimodal distribution.

Chart 2: Model of L-Estimator and Distribution of Instructional Personnel

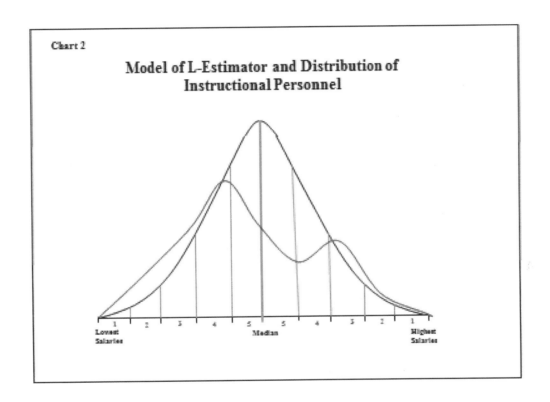

Determination of the Fiscal Capacities of Local School Districts

In order to understand the current fiscal capacities and the future outlook for individual school districts, it is necessary to understand the methodology used by Commonwealth of Virginia to assess the fiscal capacities for all school districts. Commencing with School Year 1973-74, the Commonwealth ceased use of a single measure of fiscal capacity, i.e., True Valuation of Real and Public Service Corporations and shifted to an index comprised of three indicators of fiscal capacity that is entitled, *Local Composite Index (LCI)*. Since its initial employment, several minor changes have been made to the LCI, although its basic structure has remained constant. The current version of the LCI formula is arrayed in **Figure 3**. Nearly all direct state aid, including *Basic State Aid*, is distributed to local school districts through use of the LCI.

Figure 3: Local Composite Index (LCI)

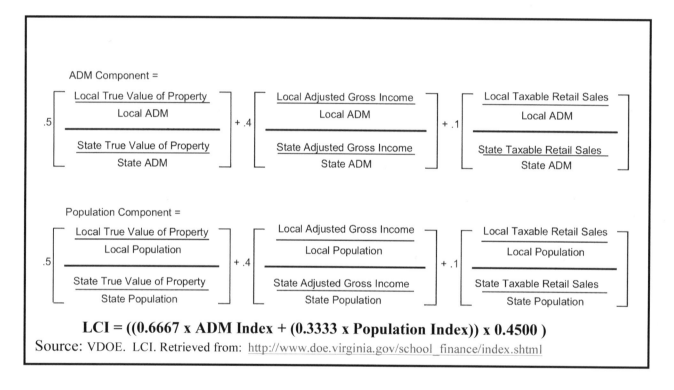

LCI = ((0.6667 x ADM Index + (0.3333 x Population Index)) x 0.4500)

Source: VDOE. LCI. Retrieved from: http://www.doe.virginia.gov/school_finance/index.shtml

Features and limitations of the LCI are presented below:

- The LCI is determined biennially for each school district by mathematically merging three separate measures of fiscal capacity: True Valuation of Real and Public Service Corporations (TV), Adjusted Gross Income (AGI) and Taxable Retail Sales Receipts (TRS). Each of the three measures is calculated as per unit ratios relative to their respective statewide averages based upon Average Daily Membership (ADM) and Population, i.e., Per ADM and Per Capita. The three measures, TV, AGI, and TRS, are separately calculated as *Per-ADM* and *Per-Capita* ratios relative to state averages. They are then weighted by 0.5, 0.4, and 0.1, respectively and aggregated into ADM and Population indices. The two indices, ADM and Population, are then merged by the application of weights, i.e. 0.6667 and 0.3333, respectively. Finally, the resulting products are summed and multiplied by the constant, 0.4500 which yields the LCIs for each of the 136 school districts. The constant, 0.4500, sets the local required expenditures for the state-calculated minimum educational costs at 45% statewide for the local school districts and the remaining 55% for the Commonwealth.

- The inclusion of *True Valuation of Real and Public Service Corporations and Taxable Retail Sales Receipts* are based primarily upon taxable revenue resources afforded the local governing agencies by the Commonwealth. That is, Virginia, through the 1971 *Constitution and Code of Virginia*, has granted the several local governing agencies the ability to tax property, real and personal, sales receipts, and several other local tax bases commonly referred to as other local revenues. The Virginia Department of Taxation equalizes real property assessments reported by localities and reports them as *True Valuation of Real and Public Service Corporations. Taxable Retail Sales Receipts* have an identical rate throughout the state, so it is unnecessary to equalize the reported retail sales receipts. The tax yields reported for the plethora of other local revenues are gained from various assessment and tax rates imposed by the localities and makes their equalization difficult for the Virginia Department of Taxation. For this reason, the Commonwealth has used an income measure, initially *Personal Income* and subsequently, *Adjusted Gross Income*, to serve as a proxy for the measurement of other local revenues, i.e., other local tax bases.

- The application of the weights, i.e., 0.5, 0.4, and 0.1, represented the average percent of local revenues, by source, that were used to fund public elementary and secondary education in the biennium, 1973-1974, however, the tax yields from the three local funding sources have changed significantly during the four decades since the introduction of the LCI and should be adjusted.

- The use of the divisor, ADM, was employed to represent education costs relative to the number of students served by each school district. In contrast, employment of the population divisor was due to a combination of political influence and the desire to address the concept of municipal overburden. Specifically, the use of the population divisor reduces the fiscal capacities of school districts that serve small numbers of students relative to their total population and generates additional state aid to school districts that possess this characteristic.

- The use of the second set of weights, i.e., 0.6667 applied to the ADM index and 0.3333 applied to the Population index was selected arbitrarily and has no rationale or research basis.

- The application of the constant, 0.4500, sets the statewide average local required expenditure at 45% and the statewide average state share at 55%. It is important to note that these percentages apply only to the calculated costs and do not represent the actual cost percentages provided by the state and local agencies. History has shown that among the 136 school districts, the LCIs typically range from 1.0000 and greater to approximately 0.1700, thereby those school districts with the 1.0000 and greater would qualify for no direct state aid while those school districts at the lower end of the continuum would qualify for 87% of their state-calculated costs. Nevertheless, the Commonwealth has historically provided some direct state aid to those school districts considered to possess high fiscal capacity and has truncated the LCIs at 0.8000, thereby guaranteeing the high fiscal capacity school districts will receive no less than 20% of their state-calculated costs for *Basic State Aid* and other state grants affected by the LCI. For FYs 2013-2014, the range of LCIs spanned from 0.1866 to 0.8000.

- Limitations of the Local Composite Index (LCI)

  1. The LCI relies on rather old data, e.g., For FYs 2013, 2014, the fiscal indicators are based on FY 2009 data while the divisors, ADM and Population, are obtained from School Year 2010 and Calendar Year 2010, respectively. As a result, the current economic conditions of localities are unlikely to be accurately reflected by their current LCIs;

  2. The LCI is a relative measure that contrasts the fiscal condition of one locality against the Commonwealth as a whole. Instead of solely contrasting overtime the changing fiscal conditions of localities, the LCI contrasts each locality against all other localities. Thus, a locality that experiences deteriorating economic conditions may see its LCI rise if a preponderance of other localities experience even worse economic conditions; and

  3. The massive concentrations of wealth, income, and sales in several localities significantly affect the LCIs for all localities and make the LCI volatile. That is, whenever the large localities, as measured by population and students, experience rapid economic growth, their LCIs tend to rapidly increase while the preponderance of other localities will see their LCIs decrease. The reverse is also true; when the economic conditions in the several large localities rapidly deteriorate, their LCIs fall and most other localities will see their LCIs increase rapidly.

State and Local Costs and Distribution Formula for State Basic Aid

- The State Basic Aid formula in narrative form is presented in three parts:

  Part 1: RLE = [((ADM x State Per Pupil in ADM) – Dedicated State Sales Tax Receipts) x LCI))]

  Part 2: State Basic Aid = [((ADM x School District Cost Per-ADM) – Dedicated 1¢ State Sales Tax Receipts) x (1-LCI))]

  Part 3: Appropriation in excess of RLE is provided by the local governing body.

- The State Basic Aid algebraic algorithms also are presented in three parts:

  o Part 1: $U_i = [(P_iF_i - G) \times V_i]$

     Where: U_i = Required Local Effort (RLE)
     P_i = Units of the $_i$th district (pupils -- March 31 ADM)
     F = Foundation program per unit value (determined by the state)
     G = Dedicated 1¢ state sales tax
     V_i = Local Composite Index

  o Part 2: $S_i = [(P_iF_i - G) - U_i]$

     Where: S_i = State equalization grant to $_i$th district
     P_i = Units of the $_i$th district (pupils -- March 31 ADM)
     F = Foundation program per unit value (determined by the state)
     G = Dedicated 1¢ state sales tax

  o Part 3: $O_i = T_i - U_i$

     Where: O_i = Local Leeway Funds
     T_i = Total Local Appropriation
     U_i = Required Local Effort (RLE)

- A *Cookbook* example of the calculation of **Basic State Aid for FY 2014** (Parts 1 and 2) for Henry County School District is provided below:[124]

Henry County School District

Step 1:	6,976.95	ADM
Step 2:	$5,169.00	Cost Per ADM
Step 3:	$36,063,854.55	Step 1 x Step 2 (Foundation Guarantee)
Step 4:	$7,273,266.00	State Sales Tax
Step 5:	$28,790,588.55	Step 3 – Step 4
Step 6:	0.2430	Local Composite Index (LCI)
Part 1--Step 7:	**$6,996,113.02**	Step 5 x Step 6 **(Required Local Effort)**
Part 2--Step 8:	**$21,794,475.53**	Step 5 – Step 7 **(State Basic Aid)**

- The Local Leeway Component (Part 3) is a simple appropriation by the governing body, i.e. County Board of Supervisors or City/Town Council.[125] For the above example, Henry County Board of Supervisors serves as the governing body. Approximately $10 million Local Leeway funds are projected for FY 2014 in addition to the Required Local Effort of nearly $7.0 million.

Determination of State and Local Funding Responsibilities and Distribution Formulae for Other State Grants, Including Other SOQ funds, Incentive Grants, Categorical Grants, and Lottery Funds

- The majority of other state grants are distributed by the following formula, presented in a two-part narrative form:

  - Part 1: RLE = [((ADM x School District Cost Per-Pupil in ADM) x LCI)]
  - Part 2: State Aid = [((ADM x School District Cost Per-ADM) x (1-LCI))]

- The other state grants as algebraic algorithms also are presented in two parts:

  - Part 1: $U_i = [(P_i F_i) \times V_i]$

    Where: U_i = Required Local Effort (RLE)
    P_i = Units of the ith district (pupils -- March 31 ADM)
    F = State grant per-ADM value (determined by the state)
    V_i = Local Composite Index (LCI)

  - Part 2: $S_i = [(P_i F_i) - (1 - V_i)]$

    Where: S_i = State equalization grant to ith district

---

[124] Data derived from Virginia Department of Education, *Calculation Template (FYs 2013, 2014).* (Richmond, VA.: VDOE, 2012). Retrieved from: http://www.doe.virginia.gov/school_finance/budget/calc_tools/index.shtml

[125] Only two towns, *Colonial Beach* and *West Point,* currently operate public schools. See: *Code of Virginia, Chapter 5, Articles 1-7,* §§22.1-28 et. seq.

$$P_i = \text{Units of the } _i\text{th district (pupils -- March 31 ADM)}$$
$$F = \text{Other grant per unit value (determined by the state)}$$
$$V_i = \text{Local Composite Index (LCI)}$$

- A *Cookbook* example of the calculation of State Special Education Grant (SOQ) for FY 2014 (Parts 1 and 2) for Henry County School District is provided below:[126]

Henry County School District

Step 1:	6,976.95	ADM
Step 2:	$462.00	Cost Per ADM
Step 3:	$3,223,350.90	Step 1 x Step 2
Step 4:	0.2430	Local Composite Index (LCI)
Part 1--Step 5:	**$783,274.27**	Step 3 x Step 4 **(Spec Educ RLE)**
Step 1:	6,976.95	ADM
Step 2:	$462.00	Cost Per ADM
Step 3:	$3,223,350.90	Step 1 x Step 2
Step 4:	0.7570	(1 - Local Composite Index (LCI)
Part 2--Step 5:	**$3,223,350.90**	Step 3 x Step 4 **(Spec. Educ. St. Aid)**

In addition to the 11 SOQ grants, with a total appropriation of **$5,194,506,961,** the Commonwealth provides state revenue to local school districts under three additional classifications: *Incentive Programs, Categorical Programs,*[127] and *Lottery-Funded Programs.* Most of the individual grants contained within the three classifications are allocated similarly to the Special Education SOQ grant illustrated above. That is, most grants are equalized by taking into consideration the fiscal capacities of the local school districts through use of the LCI. The several funds, by fund classification, are listed below with their FY 2014 appropriations.

Incentive Programs

Fund	2014 Appropriation
Compensation Supplement	$60,963,418
Academic Year Governors' School	12,271,982
Additional Assistance with Retirement, Inflation and Preschool Costs	55,000,000
Clinical Faculty	318,750
Career Switcher Mentoring Grants	279,983
Governors' School Startup and Expansion Grants	100,000
Special Education – Endorsement	600,000
Special Education – Vocational Education	200,089
Diploma Reforms – Virginia Workplace Readiness Skills	

---

[126] Data derived from Virginia Department of Education, *Calculation Template (FYs 2013, 2014).* (Richmond, VA.: VDOE, 2012). Retrieved from: http://www.doe.virginia.gov/school_finance/budget/calc_tools/index.shtml

[127] Technically, the three classifications are all categorical since the state revenue and local required match for each fund is intended to be expended for the purpose of the appropriation.

Assessment	308,655
▪ Strategic Compensation for Teachers	4,497,651
▪ Early Reading Specialists Initiative	956,068
▪ Technology – VPSA	64,290,100
▪ Social Security Equipment Grants	6,000,000
Subtotal – (Incentive Accounts)	**$205,786,696**

Categorical Programs

Fund	2014 Appropriation
▪ Adult Education	$1,036,885
▪ Adult Literacy	2,480,000
▪ Virtual Virginia	1,626,577
▪ American Indian Treaty Commitment	45,094
▪ School Lunch	5,801,932
▪ Special Education – Homebound	5,372,903
▪ Special Education – Jails	3,414,375
▪ Special Education – State Operated Programs	32,130,764
Subtotal (Categorical Programs)	**$51,908,530**

Lottery-Funded Programs

Fund	2014 Appropriation
▪ Foster Care	$8,962,411
▪ At-Risk	78,687,071
▪ Virginia Pre-School Initiative	67,424,295
▪ Early Reading Intervention	17,482,065
▪ Mentor Teacher	1,000,000
▪ K-3 Primary Class Size Reduction	103,971,881
▪ School Breakfast	3,612,556
▪ SOL Algebra Readiness	11,394,145
▪ Alternative Education	8,048,710
▪ ISAEP	2,247,581
▪ Special Education – Regional Tuition	77,774,168
▪ Career and Technical Education	10,400,829
▪ Supplemental Basic Aid	890,493
▪ English as a Second Language	45,258,661
▪ Remedial Summer School (Split Funded)	11,445,911
▪ Textbooks (Split Funded)	61,667,293
▪ Project Graduation (Direct Aid Portion)	2,774,478
▪ Virginia Teacher Corps (NCLB/EFAL)	415,000

- Race to GED (NCLB/EFAL)   2,410,988
- Path to Industry Certification (NCLB/EFAL)   1,331,464

Subtotal (Lottery-Funded Programs)   **$517,200,000**

Total (All Programs Including SOQ Grants)   **$5,969,402,187**

Displayed in **Chart 3** are percentages, by Major Classification, of the state funds projected for allocation to local school districts in FY 2014. Eighty-seven percent of the state allocations for FY 2014 are projected to flow through SOQ accounts, 8.7 percent through Lottery-funded programs, 3.4 percent through Incentive Programs, and 0.9 percent through Categorical Programs.

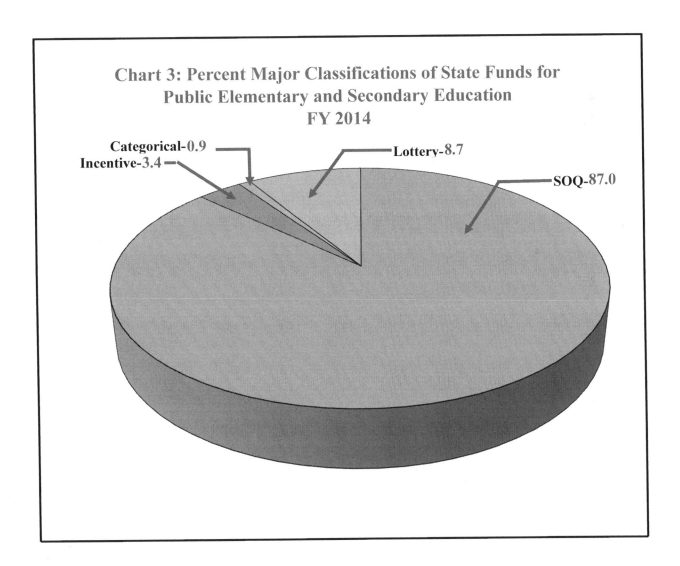

Chart 3: Percent Major Classifications of State Funds for Public Elementary and Secondary Education FY 2014

Categorical-0.9
Incentive-3.4
Lottery-8.7
SOQ-87.0

CHAPTER 5

Acquisition of School Facilities in the Commonwealth of Virginia

The following two terms and their definitions are used in discussions pursuant to the acquisition of school facilities:

Capital Outlay: An expenditure that results in the acquisition of fixed assets or additions to fixed assets which are presumed to have benefits for more than one year. The expenditure is for land or existing buildings, improvements of grounds, construction of buildings, additions to buildings, remodeling of buildings, or initial, additional, and replacement equipment.

Debt Service: An expenditure for the purpose of retirement of debt and includes bond or loan principal, interest, and service charges.

Graphically displayed in **Figure 4** are Total Expenditures, Capital Outlay, and Debt Service Expenditures per-Enrolled Pupil for the Commonwealth of Virginia, FYs 1990, 2002, 2008, and 2012. Note the decline registered in FY 2012 for Total Expenditures per-Pupil and Capital Outlay per-Pupil, although there was a slight increase in Debt Service per-Pupil.

Debt Limitation

Pursuant to the Virginia Constitution, Article VII, §10(a). Debt.

(a) No city or town shall issue any bonds or other interest-bearing obligations which, including existing indebtedness, shall at any time **exceed ten per centum** of the assessed valuation of the real estate in the **city or town** subject to taxation, as shown by the last preceding assessment for taxes. (Bold added)

The Constitution is silent on a debt limitation for counties, thereby freeing counties from a debt limitation.

Voter Approval Requirements

- Municipalities (cities) generally do not have to hold a referendum to gain voter approval for the issue of bonds, including school bonds, regardless of whether they sell the bonds on the open market or use the Virginia Public School Authority (VPSA).[128]

---

[128] A further discussion of the Virginia Public School Building Authority (VPSA) follows.

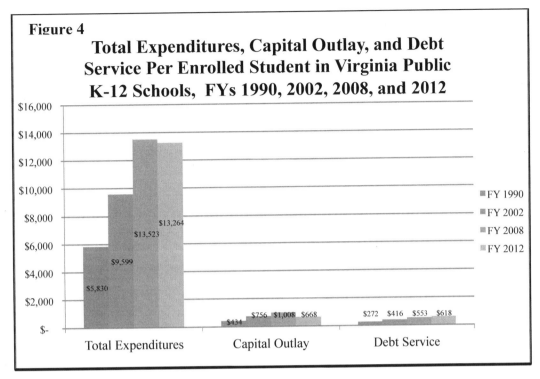

Figure 4

Total Expenditures, Capital Outlay, and Debt Service Per Enrolled Student in Virginia Public K-12 Schools, FYs 1990, 2002, 2008, and 2012

Source: Virginia Department of Education, *Superintendents' Annual Report, Table 13, FYs 1990, 2002, 2008, & 2012.* (Richmond, Va.: VDOE, 1990, 2002, 2008, & 2012).

- Counties that intend to sell their bonds on the open market are required to conduct a referendum to gain voter approval.[129] However, if the counties seek to sell their bonds through *VPSA* or apply for a loan from the *Virginia Literary Fund*, they are not obligated to seek voter approval through the conduct of a referendum.[130] In some counties, their governing bodies, i.e. boards of supervisors, have self-imposed a requirement to obtain voter approval regardless of whether they intend to sell the bonds on the open market or through the VPSA.

Virginia Public School Authority (VPSA)

- The Virginia Public School Authority (VPSA) was established during the era of *Massive Resistance*. Led by U.S. Senator Harry F. Byrd, Sr., the purpose of *Massive Resistance* was to avoid desegregation of public schools ordered by the courts following *Brown v. Board of Education, Topeka, Kansas,* the 1954 United States Supreme Court landmark decision.[131] Although the legal battle following *Brown* was concluded promptly, the battle to end segregation of public schools persisted for many years. In the immediate years following *Brown*, a large number of Virginia citizens were upset and showed their displeasure partially by denying their local school districts sufficient resources to erect or renovate school facilities. Frustrated by their inability to acquire the necessary local resources for capital facilities, leaders of both county and city school districts appealed to the Governor and General Assembly for additional state revenue to acquire and/or

---

[129] *Code of Virginia*, §15.2-2611. **Holding of election; order authorizing bonds; authority of governing body.**

[130] *Code of Virginia*, §22.1-167. **Issuance of bonds of Authority.**

[131] *Brown v. Board of Education, Supra.*

renovate their facilities. Their pleas were answered by the enactment of VPSA in 1962. The key component of VPSA permitted counties to join with municipalities to incur debt for capital construction *without seeking voter approval through referenda.*[132]

- Through statutory authority, VPSA is governed by a board comprised of the following eight members:

The State Treasurer, the State Comptroller, the Superintendent of Public Instruction or his designee, and five additional members appointed by the Governor constitute the VPSA Board. The gubernatorial appointees serve at the pleasure of the Governor for six-year terms (except appointments to fill vacancies are for the unexpired terms). The Governor appoints the Chair of the VPSA.[133]

- The Virginia Public School Authority operates several financing programs for public primary and secondary education, including the following:
  - Pooled Bond Program – Tax Exempt Financing
  - Literary Loan Interest Rate Subsidy Program
  - Stand Alone Bond Program
  - School Educational Technology Notes

- The goals of the VPSA's financing programs are to: provide market access to those communities which do not have ready access; provide low cost financing; and maintain the high credit quality to ensure that the lowest possible interest rates are obtained.[134] The Virginia Public School Authority (VPSA) was created in 1962 to provide capital to make loans to local units for school purposes, thus providing enhanced market access while minimizing costs. The program functions in coordination with the resources of the Literary Fund, a constitutional perpetual fund of the Commonwealth of Virginia for educational purposes. Authority bonds are secured from repayments of general obligation loans made to local school districts, as well as the collateral availability of repayments of similar cash-funded loans made from the Virginia Literary Fund. In addition, state aid will be intercepted in the event of a default by a local district, although the program has experienced no defaults in its 42-year history. The local loan repayments are synchronized with VPSA's own bond requirements to meet the obligated debt service. Including the cash flow from the Literary Fund loan repayments, debt service of the VPSA is covered a generous 1.41 times. Additional bonds may be issued under the 1987 Resolution if all debt service is covered 1.11 times, but policy has dictated the higher actual level. All local loans, whether funded by the VPSA or by the Literary Fund, are general obligation bonds. General obligation bonds are guaranteed by the full faith and credit of the local government. These bonds must be paid before any other debts are paid. Participation in the program is broad and the operations of the VPSA-Literary Fund should be seen as an integral part of educational policy and financing in the Commonwealth.

---

[132] *Code of Virginia, (1950),* Chapter 11, § 22.1.

[133] *Code of Virginia, (1950),* § 22.1-164 et. seq. **Statutory Requirements for Board Membership.**

[134] Virginia Department of Treasury, *Virginia Public School Authority.* (Richmond, VA.: Virginia Department of Treasury, 2014).

- Although titled an *Authority*, VPSA is technically classified as a *Bond Bank* as described below:

  A state level entity which lends money to local governments within a state, with the goal of providing funds for their infrastructure needs and access to the capital markets at competitive interest rates. A county or municipality obtains a loan from the *Bond Bank* secured by either the municipality's bond or a loan agreement with the *Bond Bank*. The *Bond Bank* pools several loans to municipalities into one bond issue. The counties and municipalities then repay the loan, and those repayments are used to repay the bonds issued in the name of the *Bond Bank*. The *Bond Bank* can obtain better credit ratings, more attractive interest rates, and lower underwriting costs than the counties and municipalities could achieve individually. The *Bond Bank* is able to pledge certain state funds, e.g. Public Retirement System, State Loan Fund, etc. as additional security for its bonds, further reducing interest costs.

The Virginia Public School Educational Technology Grants Program[135]

- The *VPSA Technology Grants* was established to provide funds to eligible school districts for educational technology, including infrastructure, software, and hardware acquisitions and replacement, and innovative programs to advance the effectiveness of educational technology.
- The program shall be administered by the Board of Education.

The Virginia Literary Fund[136]

- The *Virginia Literary Fund* was established in 1810 for the purpose of providing resources for the education of pauper children. Over the years, it has been used for various purposes; the most current has been the provision of loans to local school districts for capital construction. However, few loans have been granted recently due to the decision by the General Assembly to divert revenue designated for the Literary Fund to the General Fund.

- Virginia Literary Fund management and how constituted:

  o There shall be set apart as a permanent and perpetual fund, to be known as the *Literary Fund*, the present Literary Fund of the Commonwealth, donations to the Literary Fund, sums appropriated to the Literary Fund, all funds received by the State Treasurer and required to be deposited in the Literary Fund pursuant to Chapter 11.1 (§ 55-210.1 et seq.) of Title 55 and 2 the proceeds of (i) all public lands donated by Congress for public school purposes, (ii) all escheated property, (iii) all waste and unappropriated lands, (iv) all property accruing to the Commonwealth by forfeiture

---

[135] *Code of Virginia (1950)*, §§22.1-175.6 to 22.1-175.9.
[136] *Constitution of Virginia, (1971)*, Article VIII, §8, *Code of Virginia (1950)*, §§22.1-142 to 22.1-161.

except those items specifically exempted, (v) all fines collected for offenses committed against the Commonwealth, and (vi) the annual interest on the Literary Fund. § 22.1-142.

o The Literary Fund shall be invested and managed by the Board of Education as prescribed by § 22.1-145.

Summary

The system used by the Commonwealth of Virginia to fulfill its constitutional obligation to establish the structure and funding mechanism for the provision of public schools was presented in five chapters. Chapter 1 provided the legal background and description of the public schools used by the fifty states. Chapter 2 provided a historical review of the school finance system employed by the Commonwealth while Chapter 3 gave a description of the source of funds used to fund public elementary and secondary education. Chapter 4 provided a detailed explanation of the formulae used to appropriate state revenue for the support of public schools and Chapter 5 addressed the mechanisms used to provide resources for the acquisition of capital facilities and retirement of debt.

An effort was made to provide a manual free from personal bias, although it was impossible to resist from identifying and discussing limitations of the system used to fund public schools. This is particularly evident concerning the issue of funding adequacy, which by any measure has imperiled the quality of public schools throughout the Commonwealth.

Richard G. Salmon
Professor Emeritus
Virginia Tech

M. David Alexander
Professor
Virginia Tech

Glossary

Terminology

Adjusted Gross Income (AGI)	Federal adjusted gross income (AGI) plus any Virginia additions, minus the Age Deduction and any Virginia subtractions. The AGI is aggregated by school district and becomes one of three measures used in the calculation of the Local Composite Index (LCI).
Ad Valorem	*According to value.* The term *ad valorem* is derived from the Latin *ad valentiam*, meaning "to the value." It is commonly applied to tax imposed on the value of property. Real property taxes that are imposed by the states, counties, and cities are the most common type of *ad valorem* taxes. *Ad valorem* taxes can, however, be imposed upon *Personal Property*. For example, a motor vehicle tax may be imposed upon personal property such as an automobile.
Appropriation	The authorization to disburse a specified fund amount. Prior to the expenditure of funds by Virginia School Districts, all funds have to be appropriated by the local governing bodies, i.e. county board of supervisors, city council, or town council.
American Recovery and	The *American Recovery and Reinvestment Act of 2009 (ARRA) (Pub.L. 111–5)*, commonly referred to as the *Stimulus* or the *Recovery Act*, was an economic stimulus package enacted by the 111th United States Congress and signed into law by President Barack Obama in February 2009.
Basic State Aid	*Basic State Aid* is the major general purpose grant used by Virginia to partially fund the *Standards of Quality (SOQ)* as mandated by the *1971 Virginia Constitution*.
Budget Approval	Specific timelines and responsibilities for obtaining budget approval for operation of public schools are contained in the *Code of Virginia*. See: §15.2-2503, §22.1-93, §22.1-94, and §22.1-115. Approval does not constitute appropriation; the local school board is still obligated to obtain from its governing body an appropriation prior to the disbursement of funds §22.1-94.

Calendar Year (CY)	The Calendar Year (CY) is from January 1st through December 31st, and has little relevance for the operation of Virginia public schools, except in a secondary sense. Tax years conform to the CY calendar and have implications for local governing bodies, which may result in indirect effects for the local school district.
Capitation Tax	*An assessment levied by the government upon a person at a fixed rate regardless of income or worth.* Since it is a tax upon the individual, and not upon merchandise, a capitation tax is frequently labeled a head tax. A poll tax is a capitation tax.
Categorical Aid	Funds established for specific programs and purposes. Three classes of state funds are technically categorical, Incentive Funds, Lottery Funds, and Categorical Funds. By definition, excluding *State Basic Aid*, all state grants, including *Special Education SOQ, Vocational Education (SOQ)*, etc. are categorical since they are intended to be expended for the purpose or program that they were appropriated.
Constant Dollars	The fiscal item, e.g. revenue, expenditure, salary, etc. are expressed in dollars used at the time (year) of occurrence. In essence, the effects of inflation on purchasing power are ignored.
Consumer Price Index (CPI)	The (CPI) program produces monthly data on changes in the prices paid by urban consumers for a representative basket of goods and services. All Items CPI for All Urban Consumers (CPI-U) and the CPI-U for All Items minus Food and Energy. The latter series, widely referred to as the "core" CPI, is closely watched by many economic analysts and policymakers under the belief that food and energy prices are volatile and are subject to price shocks that cannot be damped through monetary policy. However, all consumer goods and services, including food and energy, are represented in the headline CPI.
Current Dollars	The fiscal item, e.g. revenue, expenditure, salary, etc. are expressed in dollars that are adjusted for inflationary effects as measured by changes in the Consumer Price Index (CPI).

De Facto Segregation	Patterns of racial concentrations in the public schools that resulted from housing patterns.
De Jure Segregation	Patterns of racial concentrations in the public schools that resulted from governmental promulgated and enforced discrimination, primarily in the South.
Dollars Per $100 Property Valuation	A method of calculating taxes owed a governmental agency resulting from dividing property value by $100 and multiplying the result by a specified rate. For example, if the value of real property equals $100,000 and is divided by 100, the result is 1,000 units of $100 property value. When the 1,000 units are multiplied by a rate of $1.00, the resulting product is $1,000, yielding a tax bill of $1,000. This is the term for local property tax rates used by the Commonwealth of Virginia.
Equalization Grant	Grants that are allocated to local school districts by taking into consideration their local tax-paying abilities. For the Commonwealth of Virginia, the Local Composite Index (LCI) is the measure of tax-paying ability that is used to determine state and local fiscal responsibilities.
Current Operating Expenditure	Total current expenditures by local school districts, such as expenditures for instruction, administration, attendance and health, pupil transportation, operation and maintenance, school food services and other non-instructional operations, facilities, fund transfers, technology, and contingency reserves. (Net food service also includes the value of commodities donated by the U.S. Department of Agriculture, such as those provided through the school lunch and milk programs.)
Federal Impact Aid	Established in 1950, *Federal Impact Aid* was intended to compensate local school districts for the additional costs incurred to serve the children of military and other federal employees. See: *Title VIII of the Elementary and Secondary Education Act of 1965 (ESEA)),* and 34 CFR §§ 222, et. seq.

Fiscal Dependency	An agency of government that lacks budgetary control over funds approved and appropriated for the purposes which have been assigned to the agency. In the case of local school districts, the local school board is dependent upon another local agency for all approved and appropriated funds.
Fiscal Effort	The level of taxpayer exertion generated for a specific program and purpose. In the case of local public schools, local current expenditures are divided by the total value of their local resources. The Virginia Education Association (VEA), the only institution that has calculated fiscal effort of Virginia school districts, determines local tax effort by dividing local current expenditures by the dollar value for the three measures of fiscal capacity contained within the Local Composite Index (LCI). The VEA publishes the calculations biennially in *Educational Disparities*.
Fiscal Independency	An agency of government that possesses budgetary control over funds approved and appropriated for the purposes which have been assigned to the agency. In order to meet the definition of fiscal independency, Virginia school districts would have to be granted tax levying capacity.
Fiscal Year (FY)	The fiscal years (FYs) for most state governments, including the Commonwealth of Virginia, is July 1st through June 30th, while the federal fiscal year (FY) is October 1st through September 30th.
Flat Grant	A specified fiscal amount that is multiplied by a specified unit, e.g. $1,000 times the number of pupils in Average Daily Membership (ADM) $1,000, or 1,000 ADM x $1,000 equals $1,000,000. Flat grants do not take into consideration the tax-paying abilities of local school districts.
Flow-Through Funds	State agency acts as conduit for receipt and dispersal of federal funds to local school districts. The Individuals with Disabilities Education Act is a federal statute and serves as an example for the use of flow-through terminology, 20 U.S.C. §§1400 et. seq. See specifically, Title I, Part B – Assistance for Education of all Children with Disabilities.

Foundation Program	The *Foundation Program* concept was the work of two professors at Teachers College, Columbia University, during the 1930s. George Strayer and Robert Haig referred to their state aid program as a *Minimum Foundation Program (MFP)* which was intended to equalize fiscal resources among school districts. In essence, the Strayer-Haig formula required the state to determine a level of educational services that would be offered throughout a state, subtract from the costs required to provide this level of educational services a uniform local required effort and the result would be the equalized state aid. The Foundation Program gained considerable popularity and currently is employed in approximately 80 percent of the states as their primary general aid grant.
Governmental Accounting Standards Board (GASB)	The Governmental Accounting Standards Board) is the source of generally accepted accounting principles (GAAP) used by state and local governments.
General Aid	Appropriations for public schools that may be expended for any legal purpose; see current operating expenditures above.
Great Depression	The protracted worldwide economic downturn that commenced October 29, 1929 and continued to the early 1940s. The *Great Depression* was notable for its severity, resulting in actual deflation and economic harshness, particularly among the rural poor.
Great Recession	*Great Recession* commenced for the United States in December, fourth quarter of 2007. The nation did not emerge from the *Great Recession* until June, second quarter of 2009. Unfortunately, while major private institutions and the New York Stock Exchange have recovered fully, labor has not. Particularly hard hit has been nearly all public employees, including public school personnel who are still struggling.

Hold Harmless	*Hold harmless provisions,* also known as *save harmless legislation,* are designed to protect certain classes of individuals, agencies, and institutions from the effects of new legislation. For example, if certain school districts would receive less state aid following enactment of a new allocation formula, a hold harmless provision might be stated as follows: *No school district will receive less state aid than it received in FY 2014.*
Joint Legislative Audit and Review Commission (JLARC)	The Virginia General Assembly established JLARC to perform similarly as the federal General Accounting Office (GAO). JLARC is composed of members of the Senate and House of Delegates which employ a permanent staff. Under the direction of the General Assembly, the permanent staff conducts specified studies.
L-Estimator	The *L-Estimator* is a statistic designed to reduce the effects of outliers on small sample studies. However, that is not the purpose of the L-Estimator as employed by the Commonwealth, which uses the statistic to reduce the funding requirements of public schools.
Literary Fund	The *Literary Fund* was established initially in 1810 to provide funds for the support of pauper schools. Over the years, the *Literary Fund* has been used for several purposes, including its current purpose to provide low-interest loans for capital construction of public schools. However, for several fiscal years, funds have been diverted from the Literary Fund to other funds and purposes.
Local Composite Index	The measure of local fiscal capacity used by Virginia to allocate state aid to local school districts. It is composed to three separate measures, true valuation of property of real and public service corporations, adjusted gross income, and taxable retail sales receipts that are mathematically merged into a single index.
Millage	Commonly used as a tax rate applied to property for the determination of taxes. One mill is equal to $0.001. Millage is used by most states to determine property taxes and to set the amount of local tax effort (LRE) that is mandated.
PPTRA	*Personal Property Tax Relief Act of 1998,* consists of §§ 58.1-3523 through 58.1-3536.

Prevailing Positions	Instructional and support positions, which are generated through use of the *L-Estimator* statistic.
Prevailing Salaries	Personnel salaries determined through use of the *L-Estimator* statistic.
Revenue Receipts	Assets, including proceeds of taxes, interest and dividend on investments, fees and other receipts for services provided by the government that do not incur a liability.
Save Harmless	See *Hold Harmless*.
School Year (SY)	The school year (SY) commences October 1st and concludes September 30th.
Standards of Quality (SOQ)	*Article VIII, §2, Constitution of Virginia* requires the Board of Education to prescribe standards of quality for the public schools of Virginia, subject to revision only by the General Assembly. These standards are found in the *Code of Virginia* §§ 22.1-253.13:1 through 22.1-253.13:9.
Taxable Retail Sales Receipts (TRS)	One of three measures contained in the Local Composite Index which is used to measure the fiscal capacities of local school districts. The TRS is prepared and published by the Virginia Department of Taxation. See: Virginia Department of Taxation, Annual Report (Various Years). (Richmond, Va.: Virginia Department of Taxation, Various Years).
True Valuation of Real and Public Service Corporations (TV)	One of three measures contained in the Local Composite Index which is used to measure the fiscal capacities of local school districts. The TV is prepared and published by the Virginia Department of Taxation. See: Virginia Department of Taxation, Assessment Sales Ratio Studies (Various Years). (Richmond, Va.: Virginia Department of Taxation, Various Years).

Federal Statutes

20 *United States Code Annotated*, §7703, Subchapter VIII.

Title VIII, §§8002, 8003, and 8007 of the *Elementary and Secondary Education Act of 1965* (ESEA)), and the program's regulations 34 CFR §222. (Commonly referred to as P.L. 874 and 815).

Constitutional and Statutory Provisions, Commonwealth of Virginia

Constitution of Virginia, (1869), Article VIII, §§1-12.

Constitution of Virginia, (1902), Article IX.

Constitution of Virginia, (1971), Article VIII, §8.

Acts of Virginia Assembly of the Commonwealth of Virginia, (1818).

Acts of Virginia Assembly of the Commonwealth of Virginia, (1829).

Acts of Virginia Assembly of the Commonwealth of Virginia, 1870.

Code of Virginia (1950), §58-441.48 (d). This citation is prior to the re-codification of statutes; the re-codified citation is *Code of Virginia, (1950)* §58.1-638(D).

Code of Virginia (1950), Chapter 806, 2013 General Assembly.

Code of Virginia (1950), §15.2-2503. **Time for preparation and approval of budget; contents.**

Code of Virginia (1950), §15.2-2611. **Holding of election; order authorizing bonds; authority of governing body.**

Code of Virginia (1950), §22.1-93. **Approval of annual budget for school purposes.**

Code of Virginia (1950), §22.1-94. **Appropriations by county, city or town governing body for public schools.**

Code of Virginia (1950), §22.1-115. **System of accounting; statements of funds available; classification of expenditures.**

Code of Virginia, (1950), §22.1-167. **Issuance of bonds of Authority.**

Code of Virginia, (1950), §§22.1-28 et. seq. **Supervision of schools in each district vested in school board.**

Code of Virginia (1950), §22.1-23. **Superintendent of Public Instruction, duties in general.**

Code of Virginia (1950), §22.1-253.13.2. **Standard 2. Instructional, administrative, and support personnel. A. The Board shall establish requirements for the licensing of teachers.**

Code of Virginia (1950), §§58.1-3523-3536. **Local Taxes, definitions.**

APPENDIX A: Estimated Number of Public Elementary and Secondary School Districts in the United States for 2013- 2014

State	Total	Operating	Non-operating
Alabama	134	134	0
Alaska	54	54	0
Arizona	627	627	0
Arkansas	255	255	0
California	1042	1042	0
Colorado	178	178	0
Connecticut	196	196	0
Delaware	37	37	0
Florida	67	67	0
Georgia	198	198	0
Hawaii	1	1	0
Idaho	137	137	0
Illinois	866	865	1
Indiana	370	368	2
Iowa	346	346	0
Kansas	286	286	0
Kentucky	173	173	0
Louisiana	126	126	0
Maine	235	198	37
Maryland	24	24	0
Massachusetts	524	408	116
Michigan	773	773	0
Minnesota	521	519	2
Mississippi	151	151	0
Missouri	524	524	0
Montana	415	410	5
Nebraska	256	249	7
Nevada	17	17	0
New Hampshire	175	161	14
New Jersey	605	590	15
New Mexico	89	89	0
New York	696	695	1
North Carolina	115	115	0
North Dakota	181	177	3
Ohio	1016	1016	0
Oklahoma	517	517	0
Oregon	197	196	1
Pennsylvania	500	499	1
Rhode Island	49	49	0
South Carolina	85	85	0
South Dakota	151	151	0
Tennessee	137	136	1
Texas	1229	1229	0
State	Total	Operating	Non-Operating

Utah	131	131	0
Vermont	352	286	66
Virginia	135	132	3
Washington	295	295	0
West Virginia	55	55	0
Wisconsin	424	424	0
Wyoming	48	48	0
United States	15,755	15,480	275

Source: National Education Association, *Rankings and Estimates of School Statistics.*
(Washington, D.C.: NEA, 2014).

APPENDIX B: Commonwealth of Virginia: Number of School Board Members in Each School District and whether they are Appointed or Elected

School District	# of Board Members	Appointed/Elected
Accomack County	9	Appointed
Albemarle County	7	Elected
Alexandria City	9	Elected
Alleghany County	7	Appointed
Amelia County	5	Elected
Amherst County	7	Appointed
Appomattox County	5	Elected
Arlington County	5	Elected
Augusta County	7	Elected
Bath County	5	Elected
Bedford County	7	Elected
Bland County	4	Elected
Botetourt County	5	Elected
Bristol City	6	Elected
Brunswick County	5	Elected
Buchanan County	7	Elected
Buckingham County	7	Elected
Buena Vista City	7	Elected
Campbell County	7	Elected
Caroline County	6	Elected
Carroll County	5	Elected
Charles City County	5	Elected
Charlotte County	7	Elected
Charlottesville City	7	Elected
Chesapeake City	9	Elected
Chesterfield County	5	Elected
Clarke County	5	Elected
Colonial Beach Town	5	Elected
Colonial Heights City	5	Elected
Covington City	5	Appointed
Craig County	5	Elected
Culpeper County	7	Elected
Cumberland County	5	Elected
Danville City	7	Elected
Dickenson County	5	Elected
Dinwiddie County	5	Elected
Essex County	5	Elected
Fairfax County	12	Elected
Fairfax City	5	Elected
Falls Church City	7	Elected
Fauquier County	5	Elected
Floyd County	5	Elected
School District	**# of Board Members**	**Appointed/Elected**

Fluvanna County	6	Elected
Franklin County	8	Elected
Franklin City	7	Appointed
Frederick County	7	Elected
Fredericksburg City	6	Elected
Galax City	5	Appointed
Giles County	5	Elected
Gloucester County	7	Elected
Goochland County	5	Elected
Grayson County	5	Elected
Greene County	5	Elected
Greensville / Emporia	6	Elected
Halifax County	8	Elected
Hampton City	7	Elected
Hanover County	7	Appointed
Harrisonburg City	6	Elected
Henrico County	5	Elected
Henry County	7	Elected
Highland County	3	Elected
Hopewell City	5	Appointed
Isle of Wight County	5	Elected
King and Queen County	5	Elected
King George County	5	Elected
King William County	5	Elected
Lancaster County	5	Elected
Lee County	5	Elected
Lexington City	5	Appointed
Loudoun County	9	Elected
Louisa County	7	Elected
Lunenburg County	7	Elected
Lynchburg City	9	Appointed
Madison County	5	Elected
Manassas Park City	5	Appointed
Manassas City	7	Elected
Martinsville City	5	Appointed
Mathews County	5	Elected
Mecklenburg County	9	Elected
Middlesex County	5	Elected
Montgomery County	7	Elected
Nelson County	5	Elected
New Kent County	5	Elected
Newport News City	7	Elected
Norfolk City	7	Appointed
Northampton County	7	Elected
Northumberland County	5	Elected
Norton City	5	Elected
Nottoway County	5	Elected
Orange County	5	Elected

Page County	6	Elected
Patrick County	5	Elected
Petersburg City	7	Elected
Pittsylvania County	7	Elected
Poquoson City	7	Appointed
Portsmouth City	7	Elected
Powhatan County	5	Elected
Prince Edward County	8	Appointed
Prince George County	5	Elected
Prince William County	8	Elected
Pulaski County	5	Elected
Radford City	5	Elected
Rappahannock County	5	Elected
Richmond County	5	Appointed
Richmond City	9	Elected
Roanoke County	5	Elected
Roanoke City	7	Appointed
Rockbridge County	6	Elected
Rockingham County	5	Elected
Russell County	6	Elected
Salem City	5	Appointed
Scott County	6	Elected
Shenandoah County	6	Elected
Smyth County	7	Elected
Southampton County	9	Appointed
Spotsylvania County	7	Elected
Stafford County	7	Elected
Staunton City	6	Elected
Suffolk City	7	Elected
Surry County	5	Elected
Sussex County	6	Elected
Tazewell County	5	Elected
Virginia Beach City	11	Elected
Warren County	5	Elected
Washington County	7	Elected
Waynesboro City	5	Elected
West Point Town	5	Elected
Westmoreland County	5	Elected
Williamsburg-James City County	7	Elected
Winchester City	8	Appointed
Wise County	8	Elected
Wythe County	7	Elected
York County	5	Elected

Sources: Virginia Department of Education. Commonwealth of Virginia, 2012 and Virginia Association of School Boards 2014.

Appendix C: State and Local Sales Tax Rates as of January 1, 2014

State	State Tax Rate	Rank	Avg. Local Tax Rate (a)	Combined Tax Rate	Rank	Max Local
Alabama	4.00%	38	4.51%	8.51%	6	7.00%
Alaska	None	46	1.69%	1.69%	46	7.50%
Arizona	5.60%	28	2.57%	8.17%	9	7.125%
Arkansas	6.50%	9	2.69%	9.19%	2	5.50%
California (b)	7.50%	1	0.91%	8.41%	8	2.50%
Colorado	2.90%	45	4.49%	7.39%	15	7.10%
Connecticut	6.35%	11	None	6.35%	31	
Delaware	None	46	None	None	47	
Florida	6.00%	16	0.62%	6.62%	29	1.50%
Georgia	4.00%	38	2.97%	6.97%	23	4.00%
Hawaii (c)	4.00%	38	0.35%	4.35%	45	0.50%
Idaho	6.00%	16	0.03%	6.03%	36	2.50%
Illinois	6.25%	12	1.91%	8.16%	10	3.75%
Indiana	7.00%	2	None	7.00%	21	
Iowa	6.00%	16	0.78%	6.78%	27	1.00%
Kansas	6.15%	15	2.00%	8.15%	12	3.50%
Kentucky	6.00%	16	None	6.00%	37	
Louisiana	4.00%	38	4.89%	8.89%	3	7.00%
Maine	5.50%	29	None	5.50%	42	
Maryland	6.00%	16	None	6.00%	37	
Massachusetts	6.25%	12	None	6.25%	33	
Michigan	6.00%	16	None	6.00%	37	
Minnesota	6.875%	7	0.31%	7.19%	18	1.00%
Mississippi	7.00%	2	0.004%	7.00%	20	0.25%

State	State Tax Rate	Rank	Avg. Local Tax Rate (a)	Combined Tax Rate	Rank	Max Local
Missouri	4.225%	37	3.36%	7.58%	14	5.45%
Montana (d)	None	46	None	None	47	
Nebraska	5.50%	29	1.29%	6.79%	26	2.00%
Nevada	6.85%	8	1.08%	7.93%	13	1.25%
New Hampshire	None	46	None	None	47	
New Jersey (e)	7.00%	2	-0.03%	6.97%	24	
New Mexico (c)	5.125%	32	2.14%	7.26%	16	3.5625%
New York	4.00%	38	4.47%	8.47%	7	4.875%
North Carolina	4.75%	35	2.15%	6.90%	25	2.75%
North Dakota	5.00%	33	1.55%	6.55%	30	3.00%
Ohio	5.75%	27	1.36%	7.11%	19	2.25%
Oklahoma	4.50%	36	4.22%	8.72%	5	6.50%
Oregon	None	46	None	None	47	
Pennsylvania	6.00%	16	0.34%	6.34%	32	2.00%
Rhode Island	7.00%	2	None	7.00%	21	
South Carolina	6.00%	16	1.19%	7.19%	17	3.00%
South Dakota (c)	4.00%	38	1.83%	5.83%	40	2.00%
Tennessee	7.00%	2	2.45%	9.45%	1	2.75%
Texas	6.25%	12	1.90%	8.15%	11	2.00%
Utah (b)	5.95%	26	0.73%	6.68%	28	2.00%
Vermont	6.00%	16	0.14%	6.14%	34	1.00%
Virginia (b)	5.30%	31	0.33%	5.63%	41	0.70%
Washington	6.50%	9	2.38%	8.88%	4	3.10%
West Virginia	6.00%	16	0.07%	6.07%	35	1.00%
Wisconsin	5.00%	33	0.43%	5.43%	44	1.50%
Wyoming	4.00%	38	1.49%	5.49%	43	2.00%
D.C.	5.75%	(27)	None	5.75%	(41)	

(a)   City, county and municipal rates vary. These rates are weighted by population to compute an average local tax rate.

(b)   Three states levy mandatory, statewide, local add-on sales taxes at the state level: California (1%), Utah (1.25%), Virginia (1%), we include these in their state sales tax.

(c)   The sales taxes in Hawaii, New Mexico and South Dakota have broad bases that include many services.

(d)   Due to data limitations, table does not include sales taxes in local resort areas in Montana.

(e)   Salem County is not subject to the statewide sales tax rate and collects a local rate of 3.5%. New Jersey's average local score is represented as a negative.

Sources: Sales Tax Clearinghouse, Tax Foundation calculations, State Revenue Department Retrieved from: http://taxfoundation.org/article/state-and-local-sales-tax-2014)

Appendix D

School District and Salary

School Division	Avg Salary
Russell County	36,152
Colonial Beach Twn	38,843
Lee County	40,343
Norton City	40,934
Buena Vista City	41,397
Halifax County	41,911
Lancaster County	42,441
Madison County	43,103
Amherst County	43,609
Shenandoah County	44,177
Waynesboro City	44,929
Dinwiddie County	45,107
Harrisonburg City	45,404
Essex County County	45,840
New Kent County	46,128
Culpeper County	47,252
Frederick County	47,490
Radford City	48,016
Roanoke County	48,267
Prince George County	49,658
Albemarle County	50,959
Henrico County	51,727
Virginia Beach City	53,172
Fairfax County/City	63,202
Alexandria City	70,557

Each school division displayed in Chart __ represents approximately six divisions. Approximately 36 school divisions compensate their classroom teachers at $50,000 or higher. The remaining 96 school divisions pay their teachers less than $50,000. The average salary of classroom teachers for FY 2012 was $52,115. For those school divisions that compensated their teachers at $50,000 or less (96 divisions), their average salary was $45,047, compared to $58,489 for the school divisions that paid their teachers $50,000 or more. The prevailing salary used by the Commonwealth for calculation of Basic State Aid is almost precisely the mean salary for the 96 school divisions that compensate their teachers at $45,047. Through this methodology the Commonwealth maintains the status quo, thus the salary disparities among Virginia school divisions will never be closed.

Appendix E

Average Salary of Classroom Teachers, FY 2012

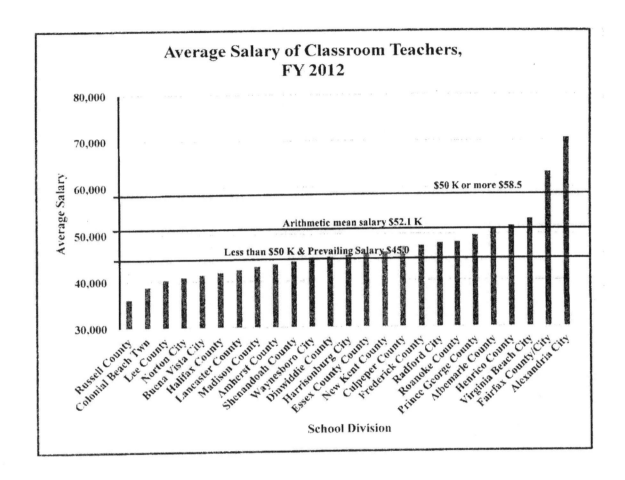